T0112368

TRUE LADIES
AND PROPER GENTLEMEN

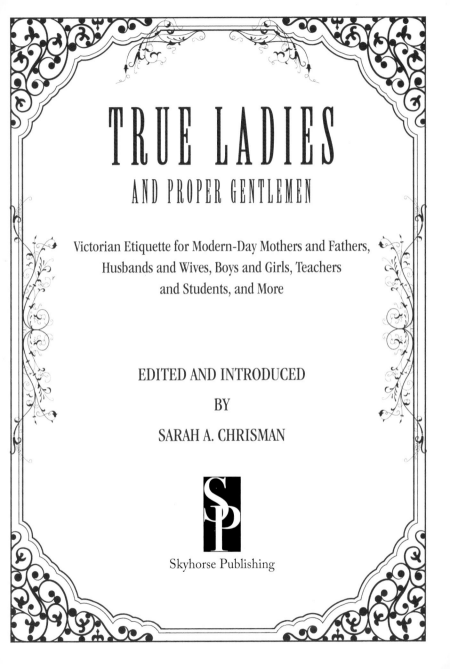

TRUE LADIES

AND PROPER GENTLEMEN

Victorian Etiquette for Modern-Day Mothers and Fathers,
Husbands and Wives, Boys and Girls, Teachers
and Students, and More

EDITED AND INTRODUCED

BY

SARAH A. CHRISMAN

Skyhorse Publishing

Arrangement and Introduction Copyright © 2015 by Sarah A. Chrisman

All rights reserved. No part of this book may be reproduced in any manner without the express written consent of the publisher, except in the case of brief excerpts in critical reviews or articles. All inquiries should be addressed to Skyhorse Publishing, 307 West 36th Street, 11th Floor, New York, NY 10018.

Skyhorse Publishing books may be purchased in bulk at special discounts for sales promotion, corporate gifts, fund-raising, or educational purposes. Special editions can also be created to specifications. For details, contact the Special Sales Department, Skyhorse Publishing, 307 West 36th Street, 11th Floor, New York, NY 10018 or info@skyhorsepublishing.com.

Skyhorse® and Skyhorse Publishing® are registered trademarks of Skyhorse Publishing, Inc.®, a Delaware corporation.

Visit our website at www.skyhorsepublishing.com.

10 9 8 7 6 5 4 3 2

Library of Congress Cataloging-in-Publication Data is available on file.

Cover design by Jane Sheppard

Print ISBN: 978-1-63220-582-7
Ebook ISBN: 978-1-63450-000-5

Printed in China

Contents

Introduction   vii

INTRODUCTION

I was grateful—although admittedly a bit intimidated—when my husband gave me a leather-bound antique book with the rather formidable title, *Hill's Manual of Social and Business Forms: A Guide to Correct Writing With Approved Methods in Speaking and Acting in the Various Relations of Life, Embracing Instruction and Examples in Penmanship, Spelling, Use of Capital Letters, Punctuation, Composition, Writing for the Press, Proof-Reading, Epistolary Correspondence, Notes of Invitation, Cards, Commercial Forms, Legal Business Forms, Family Records, Synonyms, Short-Hand Writing, Duties of Secretaries, Parliamentary Rules, Sign-Writing Epitaphs, The Laws of Etiquette, Book-Keeping, Valuable Tables of Reference, Writing Poetry, Etc., Etc.*

This book with a title of biblical length weighed five and a half pounds, had a measure from top to bottom equal to the length of my forearm, and was considerably thicker than our parlor door. My husband had acquired it for me in response to a fervently expressed desire on my part: I wanted a guide for knowing the truly Victorian response to life's daily challenges. This book certainly was that!

Targeted at a middle-class American audience, *Hill's Manual* . . . explained the intricacies of everything from how to describe a quit-claim deed for a mine (page 234) to how to give a speech upon being nominated for political office (page 465). This promiscuous array of advice covered such a wide range of human interactions that anyone from a social-climbing rail-splitter to an immigrant freshly landed at Ellis Island was bound to find something useful in the book's crimson-edged pages. The book was originally published in 1873, and by the time our particular volume was printed eighteen years later, the publishers could already boast sales of 345,000. When it appeared in the 1897 *Sears & Roebuck* catalog for $1.75, *Hill's Manual* was one of the top listings in the S & R book department—appearing several pages before the bibles.

In America of the late nineteenth century, individuals from a remarkable diversity of cultural and economic backgrounds were encountering new people and novel situations at a rate that seemed mind-boggling. Class status was a more malleable idea than it had ever been before—after all, both President Lincoln and President Garfield had been born in log cabins. In an era when it seemed a very definite possibility that the person who served as a waiter in a fine restaurant one day might well be an honored guest at the same table a week later, one of the most important things people could learn was the right way to treat each other.

The sections of *Hill's Manual* . . . I found most delightful (and most timeless) were the ones regarding etiquette—or, as the esteemed Mr. Hill put it: "What to Say and How to Do." There is a finite limit to the number of people who can find scintillating reading material in the instructions for writing a "Letter of Substitution Appended to Power of Attorney" (page 269). But it seems no loving couple could fail to be touched by the etiquette between husbands and wives—"Never neglect the other, for all the world beside," and "Let the angry word be answered only with a kiss." Turning to the suggestions about shopping, I found the first item on the list to be: "Purchasers should, as far as possible, patronize the merchants of their own town." (Shop local!) Every section on manners conveyed advice that has remained surprisingly current—even after the passage of more than a century.

My husband and I are both incessant readers, and as I explored other antique books and magazines from the nineteenth century, I found countless ways the situations described in them corresponded to the etiquette I was learning from *Hill's Manual . . .*—and still more underscoring of parallels with the modern world. *The Art of Travel* was written by Elizabeth Bisland just a few years after her 1889 race around the world against fellow reporter Nellie Bly—both of them rushing to beat the eighty-day record of Jules Verne's fictitious Phineas Fogg character. Her humorous commentary on the behavior of customs officials seems very familiar to anyone who has passed through security in a twenty-first century airport. Similarly, the first time I read the hilarious piece "Modern Improvements," about a fictitious country bumpkin's first encounter with a telephone, through my laughter I had a strong sensation of *deja vu* as I recalled the first time I had seen someone chatting with a bluetooth device and, like the grammatically challenged deacon of Belle C. Greene's story, felt certain I was witnessing the ravings of a madman. Our modern challenges and encounters are still echoing those of our nineteenth-century predecessors, and their advice on dealing with troublesome situations has a lot to teach us about our own problems.

There are reasons behind all laws of etiquette. Sometimes these reasons are obscure, but more often they become obvious if we only stop to think about them. For example: "Never use your own knife when cutting butter. Always use a knife assigned to that purpose."[1] Why? Because using your own knife in the communal butter dish smears around the crumbs of everything else you've

---

[1] *Hill's Manual of Social and Business Forms. . .*

been eating. (Besides the likelihood that your neighbors won't appreciate sharing the contents of your mouth in quite so intimate a fashion, crumbs shorten the butter's shelf-life.) Throughout all of our quotidian travails, manners keep the crumbs out of life's butter.

Some readers might be surprised to find advice from the nineteenth century about the proper way to answer an "I Saw You" ad in a newspaper[2]; or to read a story about how a woman responded to critics who said she was throwing away her college education by having a family[3]—but again, these are reminders that some issues are older than we might at first consider them.

The volume you are now holding in your hands contains what I feel to be the best of the *Hill's Manual . . .*—its portions with the most abiding relevance to society. Weight-lifters might not find this version to be quite as helpful in building muscle mass as the original (and there have been a few very minor updates of punctuation to aid in legibility), but the advice contained within is just as useful as the antique tome. To put all this advice in context, it has been interspersed with articles and stories from its own time period.

Readers familiar with antique publications might notice a charming convention that has been retained in this volume—that of separating the colored artwork as a unique portion of the work. In the 1800s, it was a common practice to print all black-and-white materials (text as well as graphics) together as the main section of a magazine and put all the color plates together at the back. Colored plates illustrating fashions would be accompanied

---

[2]   "An Advertisement in a Morning Paper"

[3]   "My Step-Children: An Echo From the Halls of Vassar College"

by reference numbers to the articles describing them, but other colored artwork would include little or no text beyond a title (if that). Women would often cut these colored pictures out of their monthly magazines and use them as decor pieces or inexpensive artwork around their home, so they specifically didn't want text detracting from the pictures. In a sweet homage to this tradition, the publishers have borrowed this formatting convention and printed the colored illustrations corresponding to the beauty advice separately, as a beautiful insert.

When I came across the story "The Story of An Old Letter" in a brittle, antique copy of *Peterson's Magazine*, I knew I had found not only a lovely accompaniment to the guidance about letter writing, but a charming way to open the book. I think we have all written missives of various sorts we regretted sending, and this fanciful story not only speaks to the universality of that particular theme but also offers a gentle segue into the idea of traveling through time via the conduit of written words—and contemplating what those words have to teach us.

Happy reading!

—S. C.

Sweethearts, Old and New

The Story of an Old Letter

By Olivia Lovell Wilson

(Fiction)

Part I. THE LETTER

It was a quaint old desk, with its numberless little drawers promising mystery, and the brass knobs that caught the firelight and winked and twinkled back at the cheery blaze. A jolly inspiriting old piece of furniture, it had never grown dim in its polished oak, with all the years that had passed over it since Rosemary Alden's grandmother sat before it, writing her epistles.

But quite in contrast to its jovial smile at the wood-fire was Rose Alden's countenance today, as she sat, her chin upon her plump little hand, discontent making a furrow in her smooth brow.

Her pen lay across a finished letter, and she knew her words had been cold and hard as the steel pen she had used.

She was not pleased with herself or the world, and least of all with the person to whom this letter was to bring gloom and despair.

She had tried to forgive him, she thought, and yet such careless neglect before marriage, when he should not have divided "a minute into a thousand parts, and break the thousandth part of a minute in the affairs of love"! What did it bode for her future?

So she said a few bitter words, and before he could explain or protest, conventionality had stepped between and they were forced to remain in mute discomfort through a long dinner given for their express honor as the happy betrothed.

He had written, the next day, too anxious to wait until they met; and pretty Rose, before her grandmother's desk, had just penned her cruel answer.

Sitting there in gloomy meditation, the maiden was so like a portrait on the wall that many people believed it to be Rose, clad in the costume of long ago. But, if one looked closely, it was not hard to discern a milder spirit in the eyes of the portrait, and a deeper glint of red in the golden hair.

This was another Rose Alden, who years ago had tasted life's first sweet pleasures, and, just as she was about to wed, had fallen asleep and been laid to rest beneath the snows.

The Rose Alden of today lifted, to her namesake's picture, eyes that were filled with tears. This Aunt Rose had been her grandmother's favorite sister, and when, years after, the little granddaughter came home to gladden her heart, she named her Rose.

Then, strangely enough, a grandson of that wooer of the first Rose had appeared to woo and win her nineteenth-century counterpart, and grandmother's satisfaction had been deep and intense.

But all this was over now! Rose began to fold her letter, when, suddenly her eyes fell upon the calendar. It was February 14th—St. Valentine's Day! The day he had laughingly said he would send her some proof of his love. And even that was forgotten! She closed her small teeth sharply, felt her grievance more than she could bear, and then a great tear fell on the folded letter lying beside its envelope, primly addressed to Walter N. Deane. Another tear followed the first, and then down went the bright head, and she sobbed aloud.

Presently she looked up proudly, dashed her tears aside, and took from a little secret drawer a small bundle of faded letters, tied with a pale-blue ribbon. Often had she thought she should look at them after love had been revealed to her, but a sweet delicacy had withheld her before; she had been too happy to think of it. Now she wondered how that other Walter Deane had written to the other Rose.

Slowly she turned over the quaintly-sealed letters, the seals broken by impatient hands that long since had folded over peaceful bosoms.

She found Walter Deane's letters and several from Rose to him. All were there together, worded briefly but full of love. Then Rose found one that made her tears fall fast; she read it twice, and her heart grew soft and more kindly toward her absent lover, yet she strove hard to retain her old spirit of defiance. Why should she attribute to this Walter Deane what his namesake never had possessed? Yet surely, if gentle Aunt Rose could say "I am wrong," might not she also be wrong and hasty in her judgment?

At this moment, Rose saw the postman coming up the street. In a second, her quick hands had dashed the sheet into the envelope. She caught up some other letters, one or two of which had been written by her grandmother, and gave them to that angel of our daily life, the penny-postman, and one more letter had gone to leave its mark upon a soul.

"It is done, and I am glad," said Rose, defiantly.

But she avoided the gentle eyes of the portrait and put the yellow love-letters carefully away, having picked one or two up from the floor, where her impetuous movement had hurled them. Then she closed the desk and left the room.

"What will happen now?" crackled the wood-fire, pleasantly; and the desk, despite its advanced age, winked from one of its brass knobs, as if to reply: "Wait and see!"

Part II. WHAT HAPPENED TO THE LETTER

Someone has said I am to tell my own tale; so here I am, and I will begin at once by saying I am an old musty love-letter. I am not going to boast of my age, for I remember distinctly Mr. Byron once said something about age being good for wine, but very bad for women; and I fancy it would be much the same with old love-letters. Still, I am led to think without egotism that I have served my time twice, as one may say after reading of my late adventure.

It was never intended that I should be mixed up with the hurly-burly busy times into which I was plunged; but I had grown very weary of the pale-blue ribbon that bound me with a small company of bosom companions, and had determined, by using one of my last sighs, to break the bond that held me, when a pretty white hand unloosed the ribbon, and after holding me a while to be read, laid me down among a number of spick-span new white ragged-edged wrappers. All were addressed, and I was returning to my well-worn folds, with the name "Mr. Walter Deane" on my yellow side, for I had always held it my duty to keep in seemly folds the contents of my written sheets, when the owner of that pretty hand laid her head upon me tenderly. I saw her weep, and then I felt that one of the new letters had hidden me from her view. Suddenly we were all snatched up together, and I felt the cold air upon me and heard a gruff voice say:

"Oh, yes, they will all get into the fast mail!"

"Ah!" I sighed, "that means the stage and coach-and-four instead of the saddle-bags-and-one."

I was very much pleased to hear we were going by the fast mail, for I was beginning to feel nervous about getting out into the world again in time to see something of it before I really got too old to enjoy myself—although, for that matter, there is a tea-pot of my acquaintance that is so old she is cracked, yet she tells me she is invited to all the fashionable afternoon-teas for miles. But then she belonged to Mr. James Madison's great-aunt, which may account for her popularity. Family blood will tell, you know, and that is one reason I've always felt I belonged to the Aldens.

But pardon this digression.

The owner of the gruff voice took us all to a big building where there were so many letters that I was sure it must be the only large place in the world where all letters come and are distributed. But I found in this I was mistaken, for I passed through others quite as large.

The parcel I was in was seized upon by a wild-eyed youth, who first read this address, then that, and flung the letters into piles in the most careless manner. I clung to my companion, a shiny envelope addressed like myself, for I feared this youth would not let me pass; for what would he know about the Walter Deane I held a message for, since he was so young? Besides, I was bewildered by many new sights and sounds, and most of all by the new envelope, which also bore my name in a clear hand.

We were soon tied up in a bundle with fifty other letters, and then thrown among hundreds in a big bag. Think of it—one in a hundred! When in my day I had gone as a select number of twelve. I must confess I did not enjoy the mixed company I was in. Wrappers blue, green and yellow—not yellow from honorable age, as I was, but a pert fresh yellow—and no seals to speak of; and one very smart pink wrapper had the impertinance to tell me that people stick their letters together by using their tongues—as if I would believe such an absurd statement! I may have looked elderly, but I'm sure I'm not a dunce to be taken in by such chaff.

We were finally plunged into a great leather bag that went together with a snap, and then the wild-eyed youth said:

"Here, Jim, you'll have to hustle this mail, or it will be behind time."

"Hustle?" thought I. Now, what does "hustle" mean? It must be a new stamp they have made. But I soon found out what it meant. The bag was taken out and hung on a long wooden arm, and soon I heard the most horrid shrieking, and, a long way off, saw a frightful-looking monster coming toward us, smoke pouring from its head and fire flashing from one huge eye.

Nearer and nearer he came, and then every fibre in my being thrilled with fear, as all at once there was a fearful rush and snatch, and we were landed all in a heap, devoured by the horrid monster, which rattled on as unconcerned about the damage—as I thought—that he had done, as if it were a daily pastime.

"There!" gasped my near neighbor. "We did catch the fast mail."

"What is the fast mail?" I asked.

A very small square epistle near me rustled about a little and said contemptuously:

"Don't you know? Why, it is the fast train that carries the mail. The Flyer, don't-cher-know? Weren't you ever on a train before?"

"Never," I replied, too amazed to be angry with the flippant tone; "there was nothing of the kind in my day."

"And when was that?" said the young Pert.

"Nigh on a hundred years ago. We moved slower then. Sweet Rose Alden spent days in penning the love-message I carry, and the quill she used was sadly abused by her pearly teeth, as she nibbled its feathers and thought of her lover. Then I was carefully folded and pressed by her dainty fingers, and a seal with a Cupid design pressed on my back. Then I was sent with a few others in a pair of saddle-bags thrown across the horse ridden by the carrier. We plodded along over mud roads and not a few corduroy ones too."

"And what's a corduroy road?" asked young Pert.

"Why, don't you know what sort of road that is? Where did you come from, not to know that?" I asked, thinking it as well to snub him a little. But at this moment my close companion spoke to me seriously.

"My friend," said he, "are you also addressed to Walter Deane?"

"I am," I replied.

"Then I have decided to sacrifice myself for the sake of sweet Rose Alden," said he, solemnly.

"Will you kindly explain?" I asked, politely.

"Yes. I contain a message of unkindness for Walter Deane, from sweet Rose Alden. Almost before I was finished, she was sorry for having written me. I am not a cold-blooded creature. The spirit of repentance had already permeated me, even though I appear stern and forbidding. Tell me: do you not convey a tender message in your bosom?"

9

"I do; but alas! It was written by one who is long since dead. I am a hundred years old."

"Love—true love—never dies," quoth my new friend. "Your message will reach him as sweetly today as it touched its owner years ago. I do not mean to reach him. Let us change envelopes; then I shall cast myself in some odd corner and be sent to the Dead Letter Office, while you shall go to him, old as you are, and take him peace. Do you agree?"

"With all delight. But you surprise me. I find the romance of the past in this day of fast mails and hustlers. Are you in earnest?"

"Never more so. Learn, my friend, that progress can never change love, because its source is infinite and omnipotent. If you agree, I will say goodbye at once and detach myself from you. Then I shall soon become a dead letter."

At this moment, I felt a pain in my side, then found myself surrounded by "hustlers." I was confused, sad, and felt my end had come, when I was suddenly handed out in the light of a broad sunbeam and heard a cheery voice say:

"Here is a letter for you, Mr. Deane."

Then I was opened by a resolute hand, and I delivered my message:

"MY DEAR WALTER: It sorely grieves me to think how I misunderstood thee yester-e'en. I am sorry. I think I was very wrong, and ask that thou forgive me. Perhaps we both were hastie. I cannot tell, but this I doe know: I love thee, and cannot live without thy love.

Ever thy own,
Rose."

The old desk winked with jovial hilarity from every corner of its polished surface, and the wood-fire crackled until it seemed to chuckle with pleasure, when in the twilight it cast its flame over the yellow paper of the old love-letter, and together Walter and Rose read again the gentle message of reconciliation.

"And you never got my other note?" asked Rose, resting her pretty chin against his shoulder.

"No, my darling. This came after your few sharp words. I thought it your own sweet mode of showing me my own fault."

"No, no; I was to blame. But I wonder where the other letter went? I must have put the old one in the new envelope. How strangely it has all happened!"

But the sweet eyes of the portrait, the yellow love-letter on the hearth, the glowing fire, and the quaint old desk all thought they understood it. Perhaps they did; who knows?

Advice on Writing Love Letters, Answering Personal Ads, Courtship, and Marriage

Letters of Love

Of all letters, the love-letter should be the most carefully prepared. Among the written missives, they are the most thoroughly read and re-read, the longest preserved, and the most likely to be regretted in after life.

Importance of Care

They should be written with utmost regard for perfection. An ungrammatical expression, or word improperly spelled, may seriously interefere with the writer's prospects, by being turned to ridicule. For any person, however, to make sport of a respectful, confidential letter, because of some error in the writing, is in the highest degree unladylike and ungentlemanly.

Honesty

The love-letter should be honest. It should say what the writer means, and no more. For the lady or gentleman to play the part of a coquette, studying to see how many lovers he or she may secure, is very disreputable, and bears in its train a long list of sorrows, frequently wrecking the domestic happiness for a life-time. The parties should be honest, also, in the statement of their actual prospects and means of support. Neither should hold out to the other wealth or other inducements that will not be realized, as disappointment and disgust will be the only result.

Marrying for a Home

Let no lady commence and continue a correspondence with a view to marriage, for fear that she may never have another opportunity. It is the mark of judgement and rare good sense to go through life without wedlock, if she cannot marry from love. Somewhere in eternity, the poet tells us, our true mate will be found. Do not be afraid of being an "old maid." The disgrace attached to that term has long since passed away. Unmarried ladies of mature years are proverbially among the most intelligent, accomplished and independent to be found in society. The sphere of woman's action and work is so widening that she can today, if she desires, handsomely and independently support herself. She need not, therefore, marry for a home.

Intemperate Men

Above all, no lady should allow herself to correspond with an intemperate man, with a view to matrimony. She may reform him, but the chances are that her life's happiness will be completely destroyed by such a union. Better, a thousand times, the single, free and independent maidenhood, than for a woman to trail her life in the dust, and bring poverty, shame and disgrace on her childen, by marrying a man addicted to dissipated habits.

Marrying Wealth

Let no man make it an ultimate object in life to marry a rich wife. It is not the possession, but the *acquisition* of wealth, that gives happiness. It is a generally conceded fact that the inheritance of great wealth is a positive mental and moral injury to young men, completely destroying the stimulus to advancement. So, as a rule, no man is permanently made happier by a marriage of wealth; while he is quite likely to be given to understand, by his wife and others, from time to time, that, whatever consequence he may attain, it is all the result of his wife's money. Most independent men prefer to start, as all our wealthiest and greatest men have done, at the foot of the ladder, and earn their independence. Where, however, a man can bring extraordinary talent or distinguished reputation, as a balance for his wife's wealth, the conditions are more nearly equalized. Observation shows that those marriages prove most serenely happy where the husband and wife, at the time of marriage, stand, socially, intellectually and pecuniarily, very nearly equal. For the chances of successful advancement and happiness in after life, let a man wed a woman poorer than himself rather than one that is richer.

Poverty

Let no couple hesitate to marry because they are poor. It will cost them less to live after marriage than before—one light, one fire, etc., answering the purpose for both. Having an object to live for, also, they will commence their accumulations after marriage as never before. The young woman that demands a certain amount of costly style, beyond the income of her betrothed, no young man should ever wed. As a general thing, however, women have common sense, and, if husbands will perfectly confide in their wives, telling them exactly their pecuniary condition, the wife will live within the husband's income. In the majority of cases where men fail in business, the failure being attributed to the wife's extravagence, the wife has been kept in entire ignorance of her husband's pecuniary resources. The man who would be successful in business, should not only marry a woman who is worthy of his confidence, but he should at all times advise with her. She is more interested in his prosperity than anybody else, and will be found his best counselor and friend.

How to Begin a Love Correspondence

Some gentlemen, being very favorably impressed with a lady at first sight, and having no immediate opportunity for introduction, make bold, after learning her name, to write to her at once, seeking an interview, the form of which letter will be found hereafter. A gentleman in doing so, however, runs considerable risk of receiving a rebuff from the lady, though not always. It is better to take a little more time, learn thoroughly who the lady is, and obtain an introduction through a mutual acquaintance. Much less embarassment attends such a meeting; and, having learned the lady's antecedents, subjects are easily introduced in which she is interested, and thus the first interview can be made quite agreeable.

The way is now paved for the opening of a correspondence, which may be done by a note inviting her company to any entertainment supposed to be agreeable to her, or the further pleasure of her acquaintance by correspondence, as follows:

148— St., July 2, 18—

Miss Myra Bronson:

Having greatly enjoyed our brief meeting at the residence of Mrs. Powell last Thursday evening, I venture to write to request permission to call on you at your own residence. Though myself almost entirely a stranger in the city, your father remembers, he told me the other evening, Mr. Williams of Syracuse, who is my uncle. Trusting that you will pardon this liberty, and place me on your list of gentleman acquaintances, I am,

Yours, very respectfully,
Harmon Williams.

Favorable Reply.

944 — St., July 8, 18—

Mr. Harmon Williams.
Dear Sir:

It will give me much pleasure to see you at our residence next Wednesday evening. My father desires me to state that he retains a very favorable recollection of your uncle, in consequence of which he will be pleased to continue your acquaintance.

Yours truly,
Myra Bronson

Unfavorable Reply.

944 — St., July 2, 18—

Miss Myra Bronson, making it a rule to receive no gentleman visitors upon such brief acquaintance, begs to decline the honor of Mr. Williams' visits.

Letter Asking an Introduction Through a Mutual Friend
912 — St., April 2, 18—

Friend Henry:

I am very desirous of making the acquaintance of Miss Benjamin, with whom you are on terms of intimate friendship. Will you be so kind as to give me a letter of introduction to her? I am aware that it may be a delicate letter for you to write, but you will be free, of course, to make all needed explanations in your letter to her. I will send her your letter, instead of personally calling upon her myself, thus saving her from any embarrassment that may result from my so doing. By granting this favor, you will much oblige,

Yours, very respectfully,
W.M. H. Tyler.

Reply

117— St., April 2, 18—

Friend Tyler:

Enclosed, find the note you wish. As you will observe, I have acted upon your suggestion of giving her sufficient explanation to justify my letter. Your desire to please the lady, coupled with your good judgement, will, I doubt not, make the matter agreeable.

Truly yours,
Henry Parsons

Letter of Introduction

Dear Miss Benjamin: This will introduce you to my friend Wm. Tyler, who is very desirous of making your acquaintance, and, having no other means of doing so, asks of me the favor of writing this note of introduction, which he will send you, instead of calling himself, thus leaving you free to grant him an interview or not. Mr. Tyler is a gentleman I very highly respect, and whose acquaintance, I think, you would not have occasion to regret. Nevertheless, you may not regard this as a proper method of introduction, in which case, allow me to assure you, I will entertain the same respect for yourself, if you will frankly state so, though it would be gratifying to Mr. Tyler and myself to have it otherwise. With sincere respect, I am,

Very respectfully,
Henry Parsons

An Advertisement in a Morning Paper

PERSONAL—Will the lady who rode up Broadway last Thursday afternoon, about two o'clock, in an omnibus, getting out at Stewart's, accompanied by a little girl dressed in blue suit, please send her address to D.B.M., Herald office?

Remarks

It is useless to advise people never to reply to a personal advertisement like the above. To do so is like totally refusing young people the privilege of dancing. People will dance, and they will answer personal advertisements. The best course, therefore, is to properly direct the dancers, and caution the writers in their answers to newspaper personals. If the eye of the

young lady referred to meets the above advertisement, she will possibly be indignant at first, and will, perhaps, resolve to pay no attention to it. It will continue to occupy her attention so much, however, and curiosity will become so great, that, in order to ease her mind, she will at last give her address; in which case she makes a very serious mistake, as any lady replying to a communication of such character, giving her name and residence to a stranger, places herself at great disadvantage. Should her communication never be answered, she will feel mortified ever afterwards that she committed the indiscretion of replying to the advertisement at all; and, should the person she addresses prove to be some worthless fellow who may presume to press an acquaintance upon the strength of her reply, it may cause her very serious perplexity and embarrassment. It is clearly evident, therefore, that she should not give her name and address as requested; and yet, as the advertisement may refer to a business matter of importance, or bring about an acquaintance which she will not regret, she may relieve her curiosity on the subject by writing the following note in reply:

The Reply
(Advertisement pasted in)
D.B.M.:
I find the above advertisement in the "Herald" of this morning. I suppose myself to be the person referred to. You will please state your object in addressing me, with references.
Address, A.L.K., Herald Office

It is probable that the advertiser, if a gentleman, will reply, giving his reasons for requesting the lady's address, with references, upon receiving which, the lady will do as she may choose relative to continuing the correspondence; in either case, it will be seen that she has in no wise compromised her dignity, and she retains the advantage of knowing the motive and object that prompted the advertisement, while she is yet unknown to the advertiser.

Great caution should be exercised in answering personals. The supposition is, if the advertiser be a gentleman, that he will honorably seek an interview with a lady, and pay court as gentlemen ordinarily do. Still, an occasion may happen to a man, who is in the highest sense a gentleman, wherein he sees the lady that he very greatly admires, and can learn her address in no other way without rendering himself offensive and impertinent; hence, the apparent necessity of the above personal advertisement.

Instances have also occurred where gentleman, driven with business, and having but little time to mingle in female society, or no opportunity, being strangers comparitively, desirous of forming the acquaintance of ladies, have honestly advertised for correspondence, been honestly answered, and marriage was the result.

Those advertisements, however, wherin Sammy Brown and Coney Smith advertise for correspondence with any number of young ladies, for fun, mutual improvement, "and what may grow out of it, photographs exchanged," etc. young ladies should be very wary of answering. Instances have been known where scores of young ladies, having answered such an advertisement, could they have looked in upon these young men a week afterwards, would have seen them with a pile of photographs and letters, exhibiting them to their companions, and making fun of the girls who had been so foolish as to answer their advertisement.

It is true that no one but the meanest kind of a rascal would be guilty of such a disgraceful act as to advertise for and expose correspondence thus, and it is equally true that the young lady who gives the advertiser the opportunity to ridicule her shows herself to be very foolish.

Personal Advertisement

PERSONAL.—A gentleman, a new comer in the city, having a sufficiency of this world's goods to comfortably support himself and wife, is desirous of making the acquaintance of a lady of middle years, with a view to matrimony. Address, in the strictest confidence, giving name, residence, and photograph, H.A.B., Station H, Post Office.

The Reply

To H.A.B.

Sir:

I am led to suppose, from the reading of the above, that it is dictated in sincerity, by a desire to meet with a lady who would be treated with candor and respect. I have at present no acquaintance to whom I am inclined to give a very decided preference, nor have I ever had any very distinct ideas on the subject of marriage. I am free, however, to confess that, should circumstances favor my acquaintance with a gentleman whom I could honor and respect, I might seriously think of a proposal. Believing that you wish, as you intimate, this letter in confidence, I will say that I am — years old, am in receipt of — annually, from property that is leased. I have been told that I am handsome, though others, probably, will have a different opinion. Of that fact, you must be the judge. I am entirely free to select whomsoever I may choose. My social standing, I trust, would be satisfactory, and my accomplishments have not been neglected. It is not necessary that I should write more. I shall be happy to correspond with you with a view to better acquaintance, when, if mutually agreeable, an introduction may take place. You desire me to send name, address and photograph, which, I trust you to perceive, would be improper for me to do. It is due to myself, and, under certain circumstances, to you, that I should be very guarded as to the manner of my introduction. A letter addressed to M.A.L., Station A, Postoffice, will reach me.

I sign a fictitious name, for obvious reasons.

Respectfully,

Nancy Hillis

Etiquette of Courtship

Whom to Marry

There are exceptions to all rules. Undoubtedly parties have married on brief acquaintance, and have lived happily afterwards. It is sometimes the case that the wife is much older than the husband, is much wiser, and much his superior in social position, and yet happiness in the union may follow. But, as a rule, there are a few fundamental requisites which, carefully observed, are much more likely to bring happiness than does marriage where conditions are naturally unfavorable.

Of these requisites are the following:

Marry a person whom you have known long enough to be sure of his or her worth—if not personally, at least by reputation.

Marry a person who is your equal in social position. If there be a difference either way, let the husband be superior to the wife. It is difficult for a wife to love and honor a person whom she is compelled to look down upon.

Marry a person of similar religious convictions, tastes, likes and dislikes to your own. It is not congenial to have one companion deeply religious, while the other only ridicules the forms of religion. It is not pleasant for one to have mind and heart absorbed in certain kind of work which the other abhors; and it is equally disagreeable to the gentle, mild and sweet disposition to be united with a cold, heartless, grasping, avaricious, quarrelsome person.

However suitable may be the physical characteristics, there are many other matters to be considered before a man and woman may take upon themselves the obligation to love and serve each other through life, and these can only be learned by acquaintance and courtship, concerning which the following suggestions may be appropriate:

Any gentleman who may continuously give special, undivided attention to a certain lady, is presumed to do so because he prefers her to others. It is reasonable to suppose that others will observe his action. It is also to be expected that the lady will herself appreciate the fact, and her feelings are likely to become engaged. Should she allow an intimacy thus to ripen upon the part of the gentleman, and to continue, it is to be expected that he will be encouraged to hope for her hand; and hence it is the duty of both lady and gentleman, if neither intends marriage, to discourage an undue intimacy which may ripen into love, as it is in the highest degree dishonorable to trifle with the affections of another. If, however, neither has objections to the other, the courtship may continue.

The Decisive Question

At length the time arrives for the gentleman to make a proposal. If he is a good judge of human nature, he will have discovered long ago whether his favors have been acceptably received or not, and yet he may not know positively how the lady will receive an offer of marriage. It becomes him, therefore, to propose.

What shall he say? There are many ways whereby he may introduce the subject. Among these are the following:

He may write to the lady, making an offer, and request her to reply. He may, if he dare not trust to words, even in her presence write the question on a slip of paper, and request her laughingly to give a plain "no" or "yes." He may ask her if in case a gentleman very much like himself was to make a proposal of marriage to her, what she would say. She will probably laughingly reply that it will be time enough to tell what she would say when the proposal is made. And so the ice would be broken. He may jokingly remark that he intends one of these days to ask a certain lady not a thousand miles away if she will marry him, and asks her what answer she supposes the lady will give him; she will quite likely reply that it will depend on the lady he asks. And thus he may approach the subject, by agreeable and easy stages, in a hundred ways, depending upon circumstances.

Engaged

An engagement of marriage has been made. The period of courtship prior to marriage has been passed by the contracting parties, doubtless pleasantly, and we trust profitably.

Let us hope that they have carefully studied each others' tastes, that they know each other's [sic] mental endowments, and that by visits, rides and walks, at picnics, social gatherings and public entertainments, they have found themselves suited to each other.

Upon an engagement being announced, it is courtesy for various members of the gentleman's family, generally the nearest relatives, to call upon the family of the lady, who in turn should return the call as soon as possible. Possibly the families have never been intimate, it is not necessary that they should be so, but civility will demand the exchange of visits. If the betrothed live in different towns, an exchange of kind and cordial letters between the families is etiquette, the parents or near relatives of the gentleman writing to the lady or her parents.

A present of a ring to the lady, appropriately signifies the engagement of marriage. This is usually worn on the fore-finger of the left hand. If the parties are wealthy, this may be set with diamonds; but if in humble circumstances, the gift should be more plain. Other presents by the gentleman to the lady, of jewelry, on birthdays, Christmas or New Year's, will be very appropriate; while she, in turn, may reciprocate by gifts of articles of fancy-work made with her own hands.

Aside from the engagement-ring, a gentleman should not, at this period of acquaintance, make expensive presents to his intended bride. Articles of small value, indicative of respect and esteem, are all that should pass between them. Should the marriage take place, and coming years of labor crown their efforts with success, then valuable gifts will be much more appropriate than in the earlier years of their acquaintance.

Arrangements for a Permanent Home

It remains to be seen whether the intended husband will prove a financial success or not. He may be over benevolent; he may be too ready to become security for others; he may prove a spendthrift;

he may lose his property in a variety of ways. It is therefore wise for the lady and her friends to see that, previous to the marriage, if she have money in her own right, a sufficient sum be settled upon her to provide for all contigencies in the future. This is a matter that the gentleman should himself insist upon, even using his own money for the purpose, as many a man has found, when his own fortune was wrecked, the provision made for his wife to be his only means for support in declining years.

Conduct During the Engagement

An engagement having been made, it is desirable that it be carried to a successful termination by marriage. To do this, considerable depends upon both parties.

The gentleman should be upon pleasant terms with the lady's family, making himself agreeable to her parents, her sisters and her brothers. Especially to the younger members of her family should the gentleman render his presence agreeable, by occasional rides and little favors, presents of sweetmeats, etc.

He should also take pains to comply with the general regulations of the family during his visits, being punctual at meals, and early in retiring; kind and courteous to servants, and agreeable to all.

He should still be gallant to the ladies, but never so officiously attentive to anyone as to arouse uneasiness upon the part of his affianced. Neither should he expect her to eschew the society of gentlemen entirely from the time of her engagement.

The lady he has chosen for his future companion is supposed to have good sense, and while she may be courteous to all, receiving visits and calls, she will allow no flirtations, nor do anything calculated to excite jealousy on the part of her fiancé.

The conduct of both after the engagement should be such as to inspire in each implicit trust and confidence . . .

Should a misunderstanding or quarrel happen, it should be removed by the lady making the first advances towards a reconciliation. She thus shows a magnaminity which can but win admiration from her lover. Let both in their conduct towards the other be confiding, noble and generous.

The Wedding

The wedding-day having arrived, the presents for the bride . . . will be handsomely displayed before the ceremony. The presents, which have the names of the donors attached, are for the bride— never the bridegroom, although many of them may be sent by friends of the latter.

The form and ceremony of the wedding will be as various as are the peculiarities of those who marry, and comprise every description of display, from the very quiet affair, with but a few friends present, to the elaborate occasion when the church is filled to repletion, or in the palatial residence of the father of the bride, "the great house filled with guests of every degree."

We will suppose that the parties desire a somewhat ostentatious wedding, and the marriage takes place in church. In arranging the preliminaries, the bride may act her pleasure in regard to bridesmaids. She may have none; she may have one, two, three, four, six or eight; and while in England it is customary to have but one groomsman, it is not uncommon in the United States to have one groomsman for every bridesmaid.

The bridegroom should make the first groomsman the manager of affairs, and should furnish him with money to pay necessary expenses.

Ushers are selected from the friends of the bride and groom, who, designated by a white rosette worn on the left lapel of the coat, will wait upon the invited guests at the door of the church, and assign them to their places, which will be a certain number of the front seats.

The bridegroom should send a carriage at his expense for the officiating clergyman and his family. He is not expected to pay for the carriage of the parents of the bride, nor for those occupied by the bridesmaids and groomsmen.

The latter will furnish the carriages for the ladies, unless otherwise provided. The invited guests will go in carriages at their own expense.

The clergyman is expected to be within the rails, and the congregation promptly in their seats, at the appointed hour. The bridegroom will proceed to the church, accompanied by near relatives, and should precede the bride, that he may hand her from the carriage, if not waited upon by her father or other near relative.

The bride goes to the church in a carriage, accompanied by her parents, or those who stand to her in the relation of parents (as may other relatives, or legal guardian), or she may be accompanied by the bridesmaids.

When the bridal party is ready in the vestibule of the church, the ushers will pass up the center aisle, the first groomsmen, accompanied by the first bridesmaid, coming next, the others following in their order. The groom walks next with the bride's mother upon his arm, followed by the father with the bride. At the altar, as the father and mother step back, the bride takes her place upon the left of the groom.

Another mode of entering the church is for the first bridesmaid and groomsman to lead, followed by the bride and groom. When in front of the altar, the groomsman turns to the right, the bridesmaid to the left, leaving a space in front of the minister for the bride and groom; the near relatives and parents of the bride and groom follow closely, and form a circle about the altar during the ceremony.

The former mode is, however, established etiquette. At the altar the bride stands at the left of the groom, and in some churches both bride and groom remove the right-hand glove. In others it is not deemed necessary. When a ring is used, it is the duty of the first bridesmaid to remove the bride's left-hand glove. An awkward pause is, however, avoided by opening one seam of the glove upon the ring finger, and at the proper time the glove may be turned back, and the ring thus easily placed where it belongs, which is the third finger of the left hand.

The responses of the bride and groom should not be too hastily nor too loudly given.

Following the ceremony, the parents of the bride speak to her first, succeeded by the parents of the groom before other friends.

Essentially the same ceremonies will be had, the same positions will be assumed, and the same modes of entering will be observed, in the parlors at the residence, as at the church.

The bride and groom, after the ceremony, will go in the same carriage from the church to the home or to the depot.

Should a breakfast or supper follow the ceremony, the bride will not change her dress until she assumes her traveling apparel. At the party succeeding the ceremony, the bridesmaids and groomsmen should be invited, and all may, if they prefer, wear the dresses worn at the wedding.

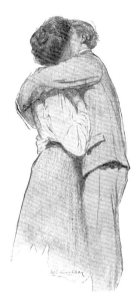

Etiquette between Husbands and Wives

Let the rebuke be preceded by a kiss.

Do not require a request to be repeated.

True Ladies and Proper Gentlemen

Never should both be angry at the same time.

Never neglect the other, for all the world beside.

Let each strive to always accomodate the other.

Let the angry word be answered only with a kiss.

Bestow your warmest sympathies in each other's trials.

Make your criticism in the most loving manner possible.

Make no display of the sacrifices you make for each other.

Never make a remark calculated to bring ridicule upon
the other.

Never deceive; confidence, once lost, can never be wholly regained.

Always use the most gentle and loving words when addressing each other.

Let each study what pleasures can be bestowed upon the other during the day.

Always leave home with a tender goodbye and loving words. They may be the last.

Consult and advise together in all that comes within the experience and sphere of individuality.

Never reproach the other for an error which was done with a good motive and with the best judgement at the time.

The Wife's Duty

Never should a wife display her best conduct, her accomplishments, her smiles, and her best nature, exclusively away from home.

Be careful in your purchases. Let your husband know what you buy, and that you have wisely expended your money.

Let no wife devote a large portion of her time to society-work which shall keep her away from home daytimes and evenings, without the full concurrence of her husband.

Beware of entrusting the confidence of your household to outside parties. The moment you discuss the faults of your husband with another, that moment an element of discord has been admitted which will one day rend your family circle.

If in moderate circumstances, do not be over ambitious to make an expensive display in your rooms. With your own work you can embellish at a cheap price, and yet very handsomely, if you have taste. Let the adornings of your private rooms be largely the work of your own hands.

Beware of bickering about little things . . . What matters it where a picture hangs, or a flower-vase may sit.

Be always careful of your conduct and language. A husband is largely restrained by the chastity, purity and refinement of his wife. A lowering of dignity, a looseness of expression and vulgarity of words, may greatly lower the standards of the husband's purity of speech.

Whatever may have been the cares of the day, greet your husband with a smile when he returns.

Be careful that you do not estimate your husband solely by his ability to make display. The nature of his employment, in comparison with others, may not be favorable for fine show, but that should matter not. The superior qualities of mind and heart alone will bring permanent happiness.

To have a cheerful, pleasant home awaiting the husband is not all. . . A man does not alone require that his wife be a good housekeeper. She must be more; in conversational talent and general accomplishment she must be a companion.

The Husband's Duty

A very grave responsibility has the man assumed in his marriage.
Doting parents have confided to his care the welfare of a
loved daughter, and a trusting woman has risked all her future
happiness in his keeping. Largely will it depend upon him
whether her pathway shall be strewn with thorns or roses.

Let your wife understand fully your business. In nearly every case she will be found a most valuable advisor when she understands all your circumstances.

Do not be dictatorial in the family circle. The home is the wife's province. It is her natural field of labor. It is her right to govern and direct its interior management. You would not expect her to come to your shop, your office, your store or your farm, to give orders how your work should be conducted; neither should you interfere with the duties which legitimately belong to her.

If a dispute arises, dismiss the subject with a kind word, and do not seek to carry your point by discussion. It is a glorious achievement to master one's own temper. You may discover that you are in error, and if your wife is wrong, she will gladly, in cooler moments, acknowledge the fault.

Having confided to the wife all your business affairs, determine with her what your income will be in the coming year. Afterwards ascertain what your household expenses will necessarily be, and then set aside a weekly sum, which should regularly and invariably be paid the wife at a stated time. Let this sum be even more than enough, so that the wife can pay all bills, and have the satisfaction besides of accumulating a fund of her own, with which she can exercise a spirit of independence in the bestowal of charity, the purchase of a gift, or any article she may desire. You may be sure that the wife will very seldom use the money unwisely, if the husband gives her entire confidence.

[M]atters that would be of little concern to you may weigh heavily on her. She needs, therefore, your tenderest approval, your sympathy and gentle advice. When her efforts are crowned with success, be sure that you give her praise. Few husbands realize how happy the wife is made by the knowledge that her efforts and her merits are appreciated.

Endeavor to regulate your household affairs that all the faculties of the mind shall have due cultivation. There should be a time for labor, and a time for recreation. There should be cultivation of the social nature, and there should be attention given to the spiritual. The wife should not be required to lead a life of drudgery. Matters should be so regulated that she may early finish her labors of the day; and the good husband will so control his business that he may be able to accompany his wife to various places of amusement and entertainment. Thus the intellectual will be provided for, and the social qualities be kept continually exercised.

Give your wife every advantage which it is possible to bestow.

Possibly the wife in social position, intellectual equipment, and very likely in moral worth, may be the superior to her husband. It is equally necessary, therefore, that the husband put forth every effort to make himself worthy of his companion. It is a terrible burden to impose on a wife to compel her to go through life with a man whom she cannot love or respect.

Betsey and I Are Out

By Will M. Carleton

Draw up the papers, lawyer, and make 'em good and stout;
For things at home are cross-ways, and Betsey and I are out.
We who have worked together so long as man and wife,
Must pull in single harness the rest of our nat'ral life.

True Ladies and Proper Gentlemen

"What is the matter?" say you. I vow! It's hard to tell:
Most of the years behind us we've passed by very well.;
   I have no other woman—she has no other man,
   Only we've lived together as long as ever we can.

So I've talked with Betsey, and Betsey has talked with me;
   And we've agreed together that we can't never agree;
   Not that we've catched each other in any terrible crime;
   We've been a gatherin' this for years, a little at a time.

There was a stock of temper we both had for a start;
   Although we ne'er suspected 'twould take us two apart.
   I had my various failings, bred in the flesh and bone,
And Betsey, like all good women, had a temper of her own.

The first thing I remember whereon we disagreed,
Was somethin' concerning heaven—a difference in our creed.
We arg'ed the thing at breakfast—we arg'ed the thing at tea -
And the more we arg'ed the question, the more we didn't agree.

And the next that I remember was when we lost a cow;
She kicked the bucket, certain—the question was only—How?
   I held my own opinion, and Betsey another had;
And when we were done a talkin', we both of us was mad.

And the next that I remember, it started in a joke;
   But full for a week it lasted, and neither of us spoke.
And the next was when I scolded because she broke a bowl;
And she said I was mean and stingy, and hadn't any soul.

And so that bowl kept pouring dissentions in our cup;
And so that blasted cow-critter was always comin' up;

True Ladies and Proper Gentlemen

And so that heaven we arg'ed no nearer to us got;
But it gave us a taste of somethin' a thousand times as hot.

And so the thing kept workin' and all the self-same way;
Always somethin' to arg'e, and somethin' sharp to say.
And down on us come the neighbors, a couple dozen strong,
And lent their kindest service for to help the thing along.

And there has been days together—and many a weary week,
We was both of us cross and spunky, and both too proud to speak,
And I have been thinkin' and thinkin' the whole of the winter and fall,
If I can't live kind with a woman, why, then I won't at all.

And so I have talked with Betsey, and Betsey has talked with me,
And we've agreed together that we can't never agree;
And what is hers shall be hers, and what is mine shall be mine;
And I'll put it in the agreement, and take it to her to sign.

Write on the paper, lawyer—the very first paragraph-
Of all the farm and live stock, that she shall have her half;
For she has helped to earn it, through many a dreary day,
And it's nothing more than justice that Betsey has her pay.

Give her the house and homestead; a man can thrive and roam,
But women are skeery critters, unless they have a home.
And I always have determined, and never failed to say,
That Betsey should never want a home, if I was taken away.

There's a little hard money that's drawin' tol'rable pay;
A couple hundred of dollars laid by for a rainy day;
Safe in the hands of good men, and easy to get at;
Put in another clause, and give her half of that;

True Ladies and Proper Gentlemen

Yes, I see you smile sir, at my givin' her so much;
Yes, divorce is cheap, sir, but I take no stock in such.
True and fair I married her, when she was blithe and young;
And Betsey was al'ays good to me, except with her tongue.

Once, when I was young as you, and not so smart, perhaps,
For me she mittened[4] a lawyer, and several other chaps;
And all of 'em was flustered and fairly taken down,
And I for a time was counted the luckiest man in town.

Once, when I had a fever—I won't forget it soon -
I was hot as a basted turkey and crazy as a loon -
Never an hour went by when she was out of sight;
She nursed me true and tender, and stuck to me day and night.

And if ever a house was tidy, and ever a kitchen clean,
Her house and kitchen was as tidy as any I ever seen;
And I don't complain of Betsey or any of her acts,
Exceptin' when we've quarrelled and told each other facts.

So draw up the paper, lawyer; and I'll go home to-night,
And read the agreement to her and see if it's all right.
And then in the mornin' I'll sell to a tradin' man I know-
And kiss the child that was left to us, and out in the world I'll go.

And one thing put in the paper, that first to me didn't occur-
That when I'm dead at last, she shall bring me back to her;
And lay me under the maples I planted years ago,
When she and I was happy, before we quarrelled so.

---

[4]   Turned down

True Ladies and Proper Gentlemen

And when she dies, I wish that she would be laid by me;
And lyin' together in silence, perhaps we will agree;
And if ever we meet in heaven, I wouldn't think it queer
If we loved each other the better because we quarrelled here.

How Betsey and I Made Up

Give us your hand, Mr. Lawyer; how do you do today?
You drew up that paper—I suppose you want your pay.
Don't cut down your figures; make it an X or V;
For that 'ere written agreement was just the makin' of me.

Goin' home that evenin' I tell you I was blue,
Thinkin' of all my troubles, and what I was goin' to do;
And if my hosses hadn't been the steadiest team alive,
They'd tipped me over, certain, for I couldn't see where to drive.

True Ladies and Proper Gentlemen

No—for I was laborin' under a heavy load;
No—for I was travelin' an entirely different road;
For I was a-tracin' over the path of our lives ag'in,
And seein' where we missed the way, and where we might have been.

And many a corner we've turned that just to quarrel led,
When I ought to've held my temper, and driven straight ahead;
And the more I thought it over the more these memories came,
And the more I struck the opinion that I was the most to blame.

And things I had long forgotten kept risin' in my mind,
Of little matters betwixt us, where Betsey was good and kind;
And those things flashed all through me, as you know things sometimes will
When a feller's alone in the darkeness, and everything is still.

"But," says I, "we're too far along to take another track,
And when I put my hand to the plow I do not oft turn back;
And tain't an uncommon thing now for couples to smash in two;"
And so I set my teeth together, and vowed I see it through.

When I come in sight of the house 'twas some'at in the night,
And just as I turned a hill-top I see the kitchen light;
Which often a han'some pictur' to a hungry person makes,
But it don't interest a feller that's goin' to pull up stakes.

And when I went in the house, the table was set for me-
As good a supper's I ever saw, or ever want to see;
And I crammed the agreement down my pocket as well as I could,
And fell to eatin' my victuals, which somehow didn't taste good.

And Betsey, she pretended to look about the house,
But she watched my side coat-pocket like a cat would watch a mouse;
And then she went to foolin' a little with a cup,
And intently readin' a newspaper, a-holdin' it wrong side up.

53

True Ladies and Proper Gentlemen

And when I'd done my supper, I drawed the agreement out,
And give it her without a word, for she knowed what 'twas about;
And then I hummed a little tune, but now and then a note
Was busted by some animal that hopped up in my throat.

Then Betsey, she got her specs from off the mantel-shelf,
Then read the article over quite softly to herself;
Read it by little and little, for her eyes is gettin' old,
And lawyers' writin' ain't no print, especially when it's cold.

And after she'd read a little, she gave my arm a touch,
And kindly said she was afraid I was 'lowin' her too much;
But when she was through she went for me, her face a-streamin' with tears,
And kissed me for the first time in over twenty years!

I don't know what you'll think, Sir—I didn't come to inquire-
But I picked up that agreement and stuffed it in the fire;
And I told her how we'd bury the hatchet alongside of the cow;
And we struck an agreement to never have another row.

And I told her in the future I wouldn't speak cross or rash
If half the crockery in the house was broken all to smash;
And she said, in regards to heaven, we'd learn to try its worth
By startin' a branch establishment and runnin' it here on earth.

And so we sat a'talkin' three-quarters of the night,
And opened our hearts to each other until they both grew light;
And the days when I was winnin' her away from so many men
Was nothin' to that evenin' I courted her over again.

Next mornin' an ancient virgin took pains to call on us,
Her lamp all trimmed and a burnin' to kindle another fuss;
But when she went to pryin' and openin' of old sores,
My Betsey rose politely, and showed her out-of-doors.

54

True Ladies and Proper Gentlemen

Since then I don't deny but there's been a word or two;
But we've got our eyes wide open, and know just what to do;
When one speaks cross the other just meets it with a laugh,
And the first one's ready to give up considerable more than half.

Maybe you'll think me soft, Sir, a-talkin' in this style,
But somehow it does me lots of good to tell it once in a while;
And I do it for a compliment—'tis so that you can see
That that there written agreement of yours was just the makin' of me.

So make out your bill, Mr. Lawyer; don't stop short of an X;
Make it more if you want to, for I have got the checks.
I'm richer than a National Bank, with all its treasures told,
For I've got a wife at home now that's worth her weight in gold.

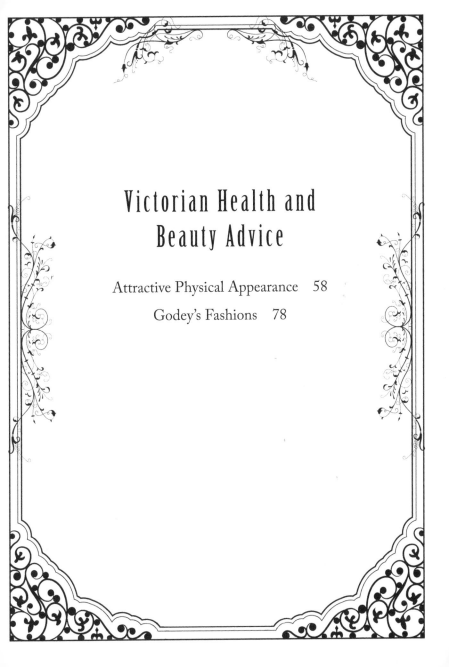

Victorian Health and Beauty Advice

Attractive Physical Appearance

Elements of the Beautiful

The love of beautiful adornment is innate in the human mind, and in reality has a great influence in elevating and refining the [human] race. It is true that the mind may sometimes be too much given to personal decoration, but the instincts which cause us to clothe ourselves beautifully are all refining and elevating in character.

The desire to please and to be beautiful surrounds us on every hand with grace, elegance and refinement.

The person who cares nothing for personal appearance is a sloven. Were all to be thus, the human race would rapidly degenerate toward barbarism. The person who is careless of dress is likely to be equally regardless concerning purity of character.

The little girl that studies her features in the mirror, while she evinces possibly a disposition to be vain, nevertheless in this act shows herself to be possessed of those instincts of grace which, rightly directed, will beautify and embellish all her surroundings through life.

The boy that cares nothing for personal appearance, that does not appreciate beauty in others, is likely to develop into the man who will be slovenly in habits, whose home will quite probably be a hovel, and himself very likely a loafer or a tramp. But the boy—the rolicsome, frolicsome boy, ready to roll in the dirt, possibly—who, under all this, aspires to appear handsome, who desires a clean face, clean hands and a clean shirt, who admires a well-dressed head of hair and a good suit of clothes—that boy possesses the elements which in the man, in an elegant home, will surround him with the artistic and the charming.

The love of the beautiful ever leads to the higher, the grander and the better. Guided by its impulses, we pass out of the hut into the larger and better house; into the charming and elegantly adorned mansion. Actuated by its influence, we convert the lumbering railway carriage into a palace-car, the swamp into a garden, and the desolate place into a park, in which we wander amid the trees, the streams of limpid water, and the fragrance of beautiful flowers.

All along the world's highway are the evidences, among the most elevated and refined, of the love of the beautiful, which, perhaps more than in any other manner, finds expression in dress.

This love of personal adornment being an inherent, desirable, refining element of character, it does not, therefore, become us to ignore or to suppress it. On the contrary, it should be our duty to cultivate neatness of appearance and artistic arrangement in dress, the whole being accompanied by as much personal beauty as possible.

In the cultivation of beauty in dress, it will become necessary to discriminate between ornament as displayed by the savage, and the science of beauty as observed in a more highly civilized life. Ornament is one thing; beauty is quite another.

To develop beauty, it is necessary to understand that the combination of a few fundamental principles forms the basis in the construction of all that we admire as beautiful. Of these are—

1. CURVED LINES 2. SYMMETRY 3. CONTRAST
4. HARMONY OF COLOR 5. HARMONY OF
ASSOCIATION

The Curved Line

A prominent feature of beauty everywhere is the curved line. The winding pathway, the graceful outline of tree, cloud and mountain in the distance, the arched rainbow, the well-trimmed shrub, the finely-featured animal, the rounded form of everything that is beautiful—all illustrate this principle. The delicately, finely rounded face, hands and general features, are essential to the highest forms of beauty in the person, and the same principles apply in the manufacture of dress. Every line and seam should run in curves.

Symmetry of Proportion

As harmonious proportions always please the eye in every object, so we are pleased with the symetry displayed in the human form and features. Thus symmetry will give a well-shaped head, a moderate length of neck, a clearly-defined nose, mouth not too large, shoulders of even height, and all parts of the body of proportionate length and size. The clothing should be made to set off the natural features of the body to the best advantage. Thus the coat should be cut as to make the shoulders of the man look broad. The dress should be fitted as to cause the shoulders of the woman to appear narrow and sloping.

Long garments will make the individual appear taller. Short garments will cause the person to seem shorter. Lines that run perpendicularly add to the apparent height; horizontal lines shorten it.

Contrast

Another feature of beauty in personal appearance is contrast, or those qualities which give animated expression and vivacity of manner. Thus the sparkling eye, clear-cut features, a color of hair that contrasts with the skin; happy, lively expression of face; graceful, animated movement of body; interesting conversational powers—all these make the face attractive by variety and contrast.

The lady's dress is relieved by flounce, frill, and various other trimmings, with colors more or less pronounced, according to the complexion of the wearer. The gentleman's dress, as now worn, does not admit of so great variety.

Very safe is it to assume that the reader desires health and beauty, and is willing perhaps to govern habits accordingly. Observe then the following regulations:

Retire suffciently early to get the necessary rest and sleep, that you may arise early in the morning.

Be sure that plenty of fresh air is admitted to the room throughout the night, by the opening of windows. Avoid feathers. A perfectly clean, moderately hard bed is best for health.

The Bath

Upon rising, take a complete bath. A simple washing out of the eyes is not sufficient. The complete bathing of the body once each day is of the utmost importance to health and beauty. Not more than a quart of water is necessary. Use the hands the same as you do upon the face. No sponge is required, and water is more agreeable to the skin when applied with the bare hand. Use rainwater; and, for a healthy person, the temperature of that which has been in the room during the night is about right. Use plenty of soap, and wash quickly. Follow by wiping the skin perfectly dry with a soft towel, and afterward give the body and limbs a thorough rubbing. The glow that is diffused throughout the face and body by this excercise is worth more in giving a ruddy, beautiful complexion than all the rouge and powder in the world.

The arrangements for this bath are very simple. There is nothing required but a small amount of soft water, a piece of soap, and a towel. No elaborately fitted-up bathroom is necessary. We have detailed all the appliances that are essential, and they are so simple that the laboring classes and the poor can have them, and be clean, as well as the rich. Occasionally, warm water, with a sponge, may be necessary to remove completely all the oily exudations from the body, but for the ordinary bath this is not essential.

The sun and air bath is very excellent for health; therefore to leave the body exposed in the sun for a short time previous to dressing is very invigorating.

Before the breakfast hour the lungs should be completely inflated with fresh air. The meals should be partaken of with regularity, while more or less of fruit, oatmeal, rice, cracked wheat, graham bread, etc., will be found necessary as a diet, in order to keep the skin clear.

The Breath[5]

The breath should be watched, lest it become offensive. Unfortunately, it is one of the troubles which we may not be aware of, as our friends may not feel at liberty to inform us of the difficulty. Offensive breath may arise from the stomach, the teeth, the lungs, or catarrhal affection of the throat and nose.

---

[5]   The recipes in this chapter are for historical reference purposes only.

Unquestionably the best remedy for bad breath is a system of diet and treatment that shall remove the cause. As a temporary expedient, when offensiveness arises from a peculiar food or drink which has been partaken of, a few grains of coffee, or cassia buds, cloves, cardamom seeds or allspice, may be used; although if the breath is very strong these will not always prove effective. It is better to remove the cause.

The following remedies for offensive breath are commended by those who have had experience in testing the matter:

Powdered sugar, ½ ounce; vanilla ½ ounce; powdered charcoal ½ ounce; powdered coffee 1 ¼ ounce; gum arabic ½ ounce. Make into pellets of 18 grains each, and take six a day. Bad breath will disappear.

Disagreeable breath arising from decay or secretions about the teeth may be removed by the following:

Rose-water, 1 ounce, and permanganate of potash, 1 grain. Rinse the mouth every three hours.

To remove catarrh, the following is highly commended:

In a pint of water put two tablespoonfuls of common fine table salt. Heat the water in a tin cup. With the aid of a nasal douche, obtained at the drugstore, or even without that, snuff about a teaspoonful of the brine up each nostril, requiring it to pass into the mouth. Use twice a day—morning and night.

For offensive breath arising from foul stomach, the following is recommended:

> To a wine-glass of water add three grains of chloride of lime. Take a tablespoonful three times a day, before the meal, and eat of simple food which is easily digested.

Another remedy for foul breath is powdered charcoal, half a teaspoonful, spread on a piece of bread, and eaten once a day for two or three days. Another is a drink of pure water, taken twice a day, containing each time 20 grains of bisulphate of soda. The taste is made pleasant by a few drops of peppermint essence.

The following is recommended as beneficial for the teeth, and effective in removing the acidity of the stomach:

> Take of gum arabic 5 drachms; vanilla sugar, 3 drachms, chlorate of lime, 7 drachms, and mix with water to a stiff paste. Roll and cut into the ordinary sized lozenge, and eat six each day.

The Skin

Beware of exterior application of cosmetics for the purpose of beautifying the skin. The greatest beautifiers in existence are plenty of exercise in the fresh air, the keeping of the pores of the skin completely open by bathing, the feeding of the body with a sufficiency of simple, healthy food, and the obtaining of the requisite amount of sleep.

It is true that sometimes a slight touch of art may improve the personal appearance. The very sallow complexion may be improved by a small amount of color applied; the hair, if naturally dry and stiff, may be kept in place by a simple hair preparation, and a white eyebrow may be brought into harmonious color with the hair of the head by a dye; all this being done so adroitly that the external application cannot be detected. But, as a rule, greatest beauty is obtained by a strict observance of the laws of health.

The following preparations, culled from De la Banta's "Advice to Ladies," are recommended for improving the complexion:

> Take a teaspoonful of powdered charcoal (kept by druggists) mixed with sweetened water or milk, for three nights successively. This should be followed by a gentle purge afterward, to remove it from the system. Taken once in two or three months, this remedy will prove efficacious in making the complexion clear and transparent.

If the skin is very pallid it is improved by a bath in lukewarm water, followed by brisk rubbing with a coarse towel and exercise in the air and sun. The pale skin is improved also by the sunshine. The rough skin is made smooth by the application of glycerine at night, followed by its removal with water and fine soap in the morning.

The skin may be whitened by the following prescription:

To one pint of water add 1 wineglass of fresh lemon juice and 10 drops of attar of roses. Mix, and keep in a well-corked bottle. Use once a day.

The sallow and muddy skin is improved by this preparation:

To one pint of water add 2 drachms of iodide of potassium and 1 ounce of glycerine. Mix and apply with a sponge once a day.

To keep the skin clear, beware of pork, cheese and other substances containing much grease. Also avoid alcoholic drinks. Keep the bowels loose by fruit and a sufficiency of coarse food. Take exercise sufficient, if possible, to produce a gentle perspiration each day; bathe daily, and get into the sunshine and open air.

The Hand

Various are the recipes for keeping the hand beautiful. If not engaged in hard manual labor, and it is very desirable to make the hands present as handsome an appearance as possible, there are a few directions necessary to keep them well preserved. Among these is perfect cleanliness, which is produced by a thorough washing, using an abundance of good toilet soap, and frequently a nail-brush.

Should the hands be inclined to chap, they will be relieved of the difficulty by washing them in glycerine before going to bed. In the winter seasons, to wash them in snow and soap will leave them smooth and soft.

To make the hands very white and delicate, the person is assisted by washing them several times for two or three days in milk and water, and, upon retiring to rest, bathing in palm oil and encasing them in a pair of woolen gloves, cleaning with warm water and soap the next morning. They should be thoroughly rubbed to promote circulation, and a pair of soft leather gloves should be worn during the day.

Should the hands become sunburned, the tan may be removed by using lime-water and lemon juice.

Should warts make their appearance, they may be removed by paring them on the top and applying a small amount of acetic acid on the summit of the wart with a camel's hair brush, care being taken that none of the acid gets on the surrounding skin. To prevent this, wax may be placed upon the finger or hand during the operation, or an old kid glove may be used, the wart being allowed to protrude through.

The nails should be cut about once a week, directly after a bath, and should never be bitten. In rough, hard labor, if it is desired to protect the hands, gloves should be worn.

But however beautiful it may be, the hand should do its full share of work. The hand that is beautiful through idleness is to be despised.

The Feet

Much care should be taken to keep the feet in good condition. The first important consideration in their management is perfect cleanliness. Some people find it necessary to wash their feet morning and evening. Many find it indispensibly necessary to wash them once a day, and no one should fail of washing them at least three times a week, and the stockings should be changed as frequently if much walking is done.

Without washing, the feet are liable to become very offensive to others in a short time. The feet of some persons will become disagreeably so sometimes within a week if they are not washed, more especially if they perspire freely.

A foot-bath, using warm water, followed by wiping the feet completely dry, and afterward putting on clean stockings, is very invigorating after a long walk, or when the feet are damp and cold.

Wear boots and shoes amply large for the feet, but not too large, and thus escape corns. A broad heel, half an inch in height, is all that comfort will allow to be worn.

The Hair

The head should be washed occasionally with soap and water. Follow by wiping perfectly dry, and afterward brush the hair and scalp with a hair-brush of moderate hardness. When the hair is inclined to be harsh and dry, a moderate supply of olive oil, bear's grease, or other dressing may be used. With many heads no oil is necessary, and with any over abundance is to be avoided. Frequent brushing with a perfectly clean brush is of great service in giving a glossy, beautiful appearance to the hair. The brush may be kept clean by washing every day or two in warm water and soda, or in diluted ammonia.

For removing dandruff, glycerine diluted with a little rose-water is recommended. Rosemary in almost any preparation is a very cleansing wash.

The yolk of an egg beaten up in warm water makes an excellent application for cleansing the scalp.

To clip the ends of the hair occasionally is an excellent plan for ladies, as it prevents the hair from splitting.

It is doubtful if a hair-dye is ever advisable, though an eyebrow is sometimes improved by a light application, to bring it into harmonious color with the hair, as is also hair which grows white in patches. There is no objection to the hair growing gray. Indeed the gray is often fully as beautiful as the former color.

Baldness is usually avoided by keeping the head cool. Women seldom have bald heads, but men often do, the baldness commencing upon the head at a point which is covered by the hat. In order to preserve the hair, gentlemen must avoid warm hats and caps, and whatever is worn must be thoroughly ventilated by apertures sufficient in quantity and size to allow all the heated air to escape. The silk hat should have at least twenty holes punched in the top to afford sufficient ventilation.

The beard is nature's badge to indicate manhood. It was an unwise fashion that ordained that the face should be shaved. Gradually men begin to learn that health, comfort and improved appearance come with the full beard, and in latter years the beard is acquiring the prestige it held in olden times. Care should be taken to keep the beard and hair so cut and trimmed that they may present a handsome appearance.

The Teeth

The teeth should be thoroughly cleaned with a toothbrush each morning after breakfast. Some persons clean the teeth after every meal, which is a most excellent habit. By cleaning the teeth regularly, no washes are necessary, though occasionally castile soap will be beneficial. Should tartar collect in such quantity as to be difficult to remove the dentist should be consulted. Should the teeth begin to decay they should be immediately cared for by the dentist. Powdered charcoal easily removes stains and makes the teeth white.

Keep the teeth clean. They look badly if not perfectly white and clean.

Regularity of Habits

It is of the utmost importance, if the individual would enjoy health and possess beauty, that all the personal habits be perfectly regular, and that attention be given to these each twenty-four hours at a regular time.

Do not let visiting, travelling or business interfere with them. You must be regular in sleep, in evacuation of the bowels, in bathing and in eating. Nature will not be cheated. She requires perfect attention to certain duties. If you attempt to violate her requirements you will certainly be punished.

Whenever the person complains of sickness he confesses to a violation, consciously or unconsciously, unavoidably or otherwise, of some of nature's requirements.

What Colors May Be Worn

Nature has her peculiar shades and contrasts, with which she embellishes all her works.

Over the retreating dark gray cloud in the east does the rainbow show itself, strong by contrast, and beautiful in the harmony of its surroundings. Surpassingly lovely are the brilliant rays of the golden sunset, as they lie reflected upon the fleecy clouds at eventide, their charm coming from their surroundings of the gray and azure blue. Dazzling bright are the twinkling stars as they smile upon us in their bed of celestial blue; and very beautiful is the rose, as it perfumes the air and charms the eye amid its accompaniments of green.

Nature thus robes all her works with shades that complement and harmonize; the result being to show the object to the best advantage.

In the higher civilization men have donned the conventional suit of black and have abandoned the domain of color to woman, who, with her keenly aesthetic nature can never be induced to forego the pleasure that comes from brilliant and harmonious hues. Alive as woman is, therefore, to the principles that make beauty, it becomes us to investigate the subject of personal appearance as affected by color.

Colors in Bonnets

Black bonnets, with white, pink, or red flowers and white feather, become the fair complexion. They also become the black-haired type when trimmed with white, red, orange or yellow.

White bonnets, made of lace, muslin or crape, suit all complexions, though not so becoming to the rosy complexion as other colors. A white bonnet may be trimmed with white or pink, but with the blonde is handomest when trimmed with blue flowers. For the brunette, preference should be given to trimmings of red, pink, orange and yellow—never blue.

Blue bonnets are suitable only for fair or light, rosy complexions. They should never be worn by the brunette.

Yellow and Orange Bonnets suit the brunette, their appropriate trimming being poppy colors, scarlet, white and black, black and scarlet, black, scarlet and yellow.

Light Blue Bonnets are very suitable for those having light hair. They may be trimmed with white flowers, and in many cases with orange and yellow.

Green bonnets best become the fair and rosy complexion. White flowers will harmonize in the trimming, but pink is preferable.

Colors for Different Seasons

Red, in its various tints, being a warm color, when worn in dress, has a pleasing effect in winter.

Purple is appropriate in winter, spring and autumn.

Green is becoming in late summer and in autumn, by contrast with the general somber appearance of dead foliage at that season of the year.

White and light tints in clothing give an appearance of coolness and comfort in summer.

Black and dark colors are appropriate at all seasons.

Colors We See First

Of a variety or color to be seen, the white or light-colored will usually attract attention first and farthest, from the fact that, most objects being of dark shades of color, it is strongest by contrast.

Next to white comes the scarlet red, which, close by, is one of the most brilliant and attractive colors. Yellow is one of the most noticeable, succeeded by the orange, crimson, blue and purple.

Colors in Dress Most Beautiful at Night

A dress of a color that may be beautiful during the day may be lacking in beauty at night, owing to the effect of gaslight; and another, most charming in the evening, may possess little beauty in the daytime. Thus, crimson, which is handsome in the evening, loses its effect upon the complexion in the daytime. So white and yellow, that add beauty at night, are unbecoming in the day.

The scarlet, orange and the light brown are also most charming at night.

Colors Most Beautiful by Daylight

Pale yellow, which is handsome by day, is muddy in appearance by gaslight. So purple and orange, that harmonize and are beautiful by daylight, lose their charm at night.

The beauty of rose-color disappears under the gaslight; and all the shades of purple and lilac, the dark-blues and green, lose their brilliancy in artificial light. Ordinarily, the complexion will bear the strongest color at night.

Colors That Harmonize

The object of two or more different tints in dress is to obtain relief by variety, and yet the two shades brought thus in contrast should harmonize, else the beauty of each will be lessened. Thus, a lady with a blue dress would greatly injure its effect by wearing a crimson shawl; as she would also a lilac-colored dress by trimming it with a dark-brown material, no matter how rich.

That the reader may understand the colors that will contrast and yet blend, the following list of harmonizing colors is given:

Blue and gold: blue and orange; blue and salmon-color; blue and drab; blue and stone-color; blue and white; blue and gray; blue and straw-color; blue and maize; blue and chestnut; blue and brown; blue and black; blue and white; blue, brown, crimson and gold.

Black and white; black and orange; black and maize; black and scarlet; black and lilac; black and pink; black and slate-color, black and buff; black, white, yellow and crimson; black, orange, blue and yellow.

Crimson and gold; crimson and orange; crimson and maize; crimson and purple; crimson and black; crimson and drab.

Green and gold; green and yellow; green and orange; green and crimson; green, crimson and yellow; green, scarlet and yellow.

Lilac and gold; lilac and maize; lilac and cherry; lilac and scarlet; lilac and crimson; lilac, scarlet, white and black; lilac, gold and chestnut; lilac, yellow, scarlet and white.

Orange and chestnut; orange and brown; orange, lilac and crimson; orange, red and green; orange, blue and crimson; orange, purple and scarlet; orange, blue, scarlet, green and white.

Purple and gold; purple and orange; purple and maize; purple, scarlet and gold-color; purple, white and scarlet; purple, orange, blue and scarlet; purple, scarlet, blue, yellow and black.

Red and gold; red, white or gray; red, green and orange; red, black and yellow; red, yellow, black and white.

Scarlet and purple; scarlet and orange; scarlet and blue; scarlet and slate-color; scarlet, black and white; scarlet, white and blue; scarlet, gray and blue; scarlet, yellow and blue; scarlet, blue, yellow and black.

Yellow and red; yellow and brown; yellow and chestnut; yellow and violet; yellow and blue; yellow and crimson; yellow and purple; yellow and black; yellow, purple and crimson; yellow and scarlet.

Hints to Parents

Give the boy a good suit of clothes if you wish him to appear manly. An ill-fitting, bad-looking garment destroys a boy's respect for himself.

To require the boy to wear men's cast-off clothing, and go shambling around in a large pair of boots, and then expect him to have good manners, is like giving him the poorest of tools, because he is a boy, and then compelling him to do as fine work with them as a man would with good tools.

Like the man or woman, the boy respects himself, and will do much more honor to his parents, when he is well dressed in a neatly fitting suit of clothes. Even his mother should relinquish her rights and let the barber cut his hair.

As a rule well-dressed children exhibit better conduct than children that are careless in general appearance. While vanity should be guarded against, children should be encouraged to be neat in person and dress.

The mother should strive also to make her boy manly. Possibly, as a pet, her boy has in infancy had his hair curled. Even now, when he is six or eight years of age, the curls look very pretty. But the mother must forego her further pleasure in the curls; for the boy, to take his place along with the others, to run and jump, to grow manly and strong, must wear short hair. His mother can no longer dress it like a girl's. It will be necessary to cut off his curls.

Godey's Fashions

*Editor's note: This list corresponds to the color insert and is presented as a separate list according to the custom of the nineteenth-century regarding fashion plates. **Godey's Lady's Book**, the journal from which they are borrowed, was the leading woman's fashion magazine of the Victorian era. At this time, the word "costume" was still being used in its French sense to denote a suit of clothing.*

September 1889:

Fig. 1. Walking costume of grey camel's hair. The lower skirt is plain, trimmed with several rows of narrow silver braid; the over-skirt upon the right side is carried up from the edge of the skirt to the bodice, and trimmed with embroidery in gold and silver; it is also trimmed with narrow silver braid. Bodice plaited upon the right side, draped upon the left with embroidery, which comes down and forms a basque below the waist. Sleeves trimmed to correspond; belt and buckle. Straw bonnet.

Fig. 2. Garden fête toilette. The gown is of white and blue crêpe de chine. The underskirt is of white, embroidered in blue; the straight gown is of blue, displaying the white in front of skirt and vest. The bodice and sleeves are slightly full, with cuffs, collar and plaited belt of velvet of a darker shade. Bonnet of plaited tulle, trimmed with flowers.

October 1889:

Fig. 1. Ulster of dark blue cloth, belted into the waist, with shoulder cape. Felt trimmed with silk, velvet and feather aigrette.

Fig. 2. Walking costume for lady, made of cloth. The front part of the skirt, full vest front, and lower part of sleeves are of plaid, which comes with the costume. Straight skirt, with revers turned back. Hat of velvet, trimmed with feathers, and small birds inside the brim.

November 1889:

Fig. 1. Carriage costume of velvet made with jacket. The skirt of costume is edged with a band of fur, slightly draped from the left side. The jacket has the front trimmed with passementerie and a band of fur around the neck and sleeves. Toque of velvet trimmed with an aigrette.

Fig. 2. Visiting costume of cloth; the skirt of gown is plain. The long cloak, also of cloth, is made of plaits and trimmed with bands of passementerie, it is lined with quilted satin. Bonnet of cloth, trimmed with jet coronet and aigrette.

January 1890:

Fig. 1. Walking costume of blue cloth, the skirt is plaid laid in plaits with slight drapery in front and back. It is braided, with side panels, vest and revers of black Astrakhan. The bodice is straight in front and finished with a belt, cut with a princess back. Hat of velvet trimmed with feathers.

Fig. 2. Walking costume of plaid cloth and plain. The front of underskirt is of the plain material trimmed with four rows of velvet. The skirt of plaid is laid down in box plaits, bound with brown velvet. Coat bodice with vest of cloth bound with velvet, velvet buttons, and velvet revers. Hat of felt, bound and trimmed with velvet and aigrette.

February 1890:

Fig. 1. Cloak of green and black cloth, damassee trimmed, with a band of black monkey fur. Toque of velvet, trimmed with velvet and jet ornament.

Fig. 2. Carriage cloak of dark maroon plush and crushed strawberry embroidered satin. The cloak is trimmed with very handsome passementerie, with a narrow band of fur edging the fronts, and a deep fur collar. The front is made entirely of satin, and is tight fitting. Large hat of velvet, trimmed with feathers.

March 1890:

Fig. 1. Walking costume of cloth, the skirt and front of bodice are in one, with deep border around the skirt and up the sides, of heavy passementerie. Over-jacket entirely covered with passementerie, plain sleeves with cuffs to correspond. Toque of cloth, trimmed with passementerie, ribbon loops and wings.

Fig. 2. Walking costume of black and green cloth. The front is entirely of black satin, trimmed with bands of green[6]. The coat is straight down, trimmed with fur down the front, and across the front to the sides. Felt bonnet, trimmed with ribbon and aigrette.

April 1890:

Fig. 1. Walking costume of terra-cotta, the skirt is plaited with a deep border embroidered around the edge, revers of velvet with buttons upon it down the right side of the skirt. Round full bodice

---

[6]   N.B. The green in the original fashion plate faded to brown in the antique illustration.

with over-jacket of the material embroidered. Full sleeves divided by embroidered band and velvet cuff. Straw hat trimmed with ribbon the same shade as gown.

Fig. 2. Afternoon gown, made of surah silk. The skirt and bodice are in one; plain skirt with the front embroidered and trimmed down each side with lace. The front of bodice is trimmed to correspond; deep cuffs of lace upon the sleeves.

Etiquette in the Home

Etiquette in the Home: Parents and Children

In temperament, physical chracteristics, mental development and moral inclination, the child is what it has been made by inheritance and the training it has received since infancy. Born of parents happy in disposition, harmonious in conjugal relation, and pleasant in circumstances, the child will as certainly be as sweet in temper as that sweet fluid which flows from a maple tree. More especially will this be true if the child was welcome, and the days of the mother prior to its birth were full of sunshine and gladness.

If, on the contrary, a badly-developed and unhappy parentage has marked the child, then a correspondingly unfortunate organization of mind and unhappy disposition will present itself for discipline and training.

Fortunate is it for the parent who can understand the cause of the child's predilections thus in the beginning. As with the teacher, when the causes that affect the child's mind are understood, the correct system of government to be pursued is then more easily comprehended. The result of this early appreciation of the case is to teach the parent and teacher that, whatever may be the manifestations of mind with the child, it should never be blamed. This is a fundamental principle necessary to be understood by any person who would be successful in government.

When thoroughly imbued with that understanding, kindness and love will take the place of anger and hatred, and discipline can be commenced aright.

One of the first things that the child should understand is that it must implicitly obey. The parent should, therefore, be very careful to give only such commands as ought to be followed, and then carefully observe that the order is strictly but kindly enforced.

To always secure obedience without trouble, it is of the utmost importance that the parent be firm. For the parent to refuse a request of the child without due consideration, and soon afterward, through the child's importunities, grant the request, is to very soon lose command. The parent should carefully consider the request, and if it is to be denied the child should feel that the denial is the result of the best judgement, and is not dictated by momentary impatience or petulance. A child soon learns to discriminate between the various moods of the fickle parent, and very soon loses respect for government that is not discrete, careful and just.

If a command is disobeyed, parents should never threaten what they will do if the order is disobeyed again, but at once withold, quietly, yet firmly and pleasantly, some pleasure from the child in consequence of the disobedience. The punishment should be very seldom, if ever, the infliction of bodily pain. A slight deprivation of some pleasure—it may be very slight, but sufficient to teach the child that it must obey—will be of great service to its future discipline and government by the parent. Commencing thus when the child is very young, treating it always tenderly and kindly, with mild and loving words, it will grow to womanhood or manhood an honor to the parents.

What Parents Should Never Do

Never speak harshly to a child.

Never use disrespectful names.

Never use profane or vulgar words in the presence of a child.

Do not be so cold and austere as to drive your child from you.

Never misrepresent. If you falsify the child will learn to deceive also.

Never withold praise when the child deserves it. Commendation is one of the sweetest pleasures of childhood.

Never waken your children before they have completed their natural slumbers in the morning. See that they retire early, and thus have the requisite time for sleep. Children require more sleep than older persons. The time will come soon enough when care and trouble will compel them to waken in the early morning. Let them sleep while they can.

Do not reproach a child for a mistake which was made with a good motive at the time. Freely forgive, wisely counsel, and the child will thus be taught that there is no danger in telling the truth.

Never give your children money indiscriminately to spend for their own use. However wealthy you may be teach the child the value of money by requiring it to earn it in some manner.

Commencing young, let the child perform simple duties requiring labor, which the parent may reward by pennies and very small sums. Let the child thus spend only money of its own earning. The boy who thus early learns by labor the value of a dollar knows how to accumulate the same in after-life, and how to save it.

Never demean yourself by getting angry and whipping a child. The very fact of your punishing in anger arouses the evil nature of the child. Some day the punishment thus inflicted will react upon yourself.

What Parents Should Do

Always speak in a pleasant voice.

Teach your children how to work; how to obtain a living by their
own efforts. Teach them the nobility and the dignity of labor,
that they may respect and honor the producer.

Explain the reason why. The child is a little walking interrogation point. To it all is new. Explain the reason. Your boy will some day repay the trouble by teaching it to some other child.

Teach your children the evil of secret vice, and the consequence of using tobacco and spirituous liquors; teach them to be temperate, orderly, punctual, prompt, truthful, neat, faithful and honest.

Encourage your child to be careful of personal appearance;to return every tool to its place; to always pay debts promptly; to never shirk a duty; to do an equal share, and to always live up to an agreement.

Teach your children to confide in you by conference together. Tell them your plans, and sometimes ask their advice; they will thus open their hearts to you and will ask your advice. The girl who tells all her heart to her mother has a shield and a protection about her which can only come with a mother's advice and counsel.

Give your children your confidence in the affairs of business. They will thus take interest, and become co-workers with you. If you enlist their respect then their sympathy and cooperation, they will quite likely remain to take up your work when you have done and will go ahead perfecting what you have commenced.

If you are a farmer do not overwork your children, and thus by a hard and dreary life drive them off to the cities. Arise at a reasonable hour in the morning, take an hour's rest after meals, and quit at five or six o'clock in the afternoon. Let the young people, in games and other amusements, have a happy time during the remainder of the day. There is no reason why a farmer's family should be deprived of recreation and amusement more than others.

Teach your children those things which they will need when they become men and women. Think what a man and woman need to know in order to be healthy, happy, prosperous and successful, and teach them that.

Etiquette in the School.

School Days

My Step-Children: An Echo From the Halls of Vassar College

(Fiction)

Cousin Esther dismissed one suitor because he was an inveterate smoker, and the smell of tobacco made her sick, and another on account of his convivial habits.[7] The third one was too fond of baseball, and the fourth would talk slang. She left them all,

---

[7] "Convivial habits"—i.e., drinking

went to college and graduated with honors, after which she went into business with her father whose health was failing. After her father's decease she sold the business, and astonished her friends by marrying Mr. Marchant, a widower with seven children.

"Poor dear Esther! She has thrown away her college education," said one.

"Worse still, she has thrown herself away," said another.

Esther told me the story as we sat together in the soft evening twilight, and I will give it in her own words as nearly as possible.

Our home-coming from the wedding journey was unexpected at the time. The house had a sombre aspect, and the children, baby excepted, were clad in mourning garments. My husband's aunt took charge of the household after the mother died, and she constantly reminded them of their bereavement. "Poor child," she would say in sad tones, when she spoke to them, yet her rule was very strict. There must be no laughter, no play. The piano was locked and no singing was allowed, unless it might be nurse crooning over some sad old song to baby. Visits and visitors were alike tabooed. The children looked pale and sad, and though they brightened up a little bit to welcome us home and seemed glad to see their father, it soon passed and they were dull and spiritless.

Aunt Jane resigned graciously and gracefully went away. As early as possible I began to revolutionize the ways of the household, for I soon found that these children were neither healthy nor happy. No appetite in the morning, no breakfast perhaps, school-life burdensome, study a weariness. They were so frequently too ill to go to school, it was impossible for them to keep up with their classes, and though bright children they were deficient.

We called a family council at which the eldest children, Imogen and Myra were present, and discussed the necessity of immediate changes. The old servants were wedded to their old ways, so we let them go and supplied their places with others more docile. We let the light, sunshine and fresh air into every part of the house; dicarded all the black garments and let the children choose the colors they would like to wear. The piano was unlocked and tuned, and we sung hymns together morning and evening.

In changing the diet we proceded very cautiously, my husband nobly seconding all my efforts. One morning when we met at the breakfast table there was a bright copper kettle of boiling water, a tray of small cups and saucers, and a dish of lemons near my place, and on the rest of the table only a few odorless flowers. Each one received a cup of hot water in which there was a slight dash of lemon juice; and Mr. Marchant explained to the younger ones how to take it. Then he diverted them with accounts of odd and laughable incidents that occurred during our recent journey. Herbert laughed, and was immediately rebuked by Lizette, our fourteen-year-old, in the name of Aunt Jane.

"Aunt Jane was very kind to come and take care of us when we had no one, and we are all grateful to her for all the good she did, and wish her happiness," said Mr. Marchant. "She has gone home now and we have other rules as you see."

"Is it not wrong to laugh, Papa?" Inquired Lizette.

"Certainly not, dear, when Papa is telling you a funny story."

It was a treat to see the brown eyes sparkle, and the sweet smile as she no longer felt repressed by cast iron rules.

Was it this repression that made the children ill? Only in part. Diet had much to do with it. They had always eaten rich and stimulating food, and in making changes I had to proceed with caution and gentle firmness. The hot water was the only innovation at that time. The usual matutinal[8] dishes, with hot cakes and coffee followed. At the other meals there was no change.

Another morning we found upon the table two large dishes of grapes with a vase of flowers between them. Sometimes we had pears, sometimes apples, later on when Florida oranges came we had those for the first course. Then we had a cereal. Crushed wheat was the favorite, eaten with rich Alderney cream. We occasionally used pearled wheat, wheatena, oatmeal, etc., sometimes hominey.

Very gradually the old rich dishes disappeared, and we had nice chops, broiled beafsteak, boiled mutton with caper sauce, roast beef and lamb, fish and poultry, with a variety of vegetables. Our desserts too were simple, yet very palatable. No rich puddings and no highly flavored sauces were allowed. We also substituted cracked cocoa for coffee. It was not easy to make all these changes in the face of life long appetites and prejudices, but it was done gently and kindly, and the good effects were ere long visible in the improved health of the children.

No amusements had been allowed because they were in mourning. I began with music. Those who could play took turns presiding at the piano, while all joined in singing some simple tune. They were soon ready to learn new songs; to sing accurately from notes, to keep time and not try to out-do each other. It brought them together socially, and accustomed them to act together in unity. We sometimes sung while waiting for meals to be ready, and also while changes were made between courses.

Herbert was a bright and nervous boy of eight, with a brain too large for his body, and often troubled with insomnia. His hour

8   "Matutinal"—morning

for retiring was eight, and in order to insure him a good refreshing sleep, we all joined in some lively game, no matter how old fashioned it was, if it was new to him he enjoyed it with a zest that communicated itself to the entire circle. One evening when some near friends of the family were with us, I proposed that we should dance Luby.

"We do not know Luby, and we cannot dance," was the chorus.

"So much the better," said I. "All stand in a circle and join hands." Mr. Marchant sat down at the piano, and touching the keys gently, sang softly. I joined the circle of children, only the younger ones would try, and said, "Do as I do." We danced around together singing in every possible variety of voice and tune:

"Shall we dance Luby, Luby, Shall we dance Luby light?
Yes, we'll dance Luby, Luby, Sweet as a Saturday night."

Then standing still we dropped hands and sung:

"Put your right hand in,"

Suiting the action to the word,

"Put your right hand out,
Shake your right hand a little,
And turn yourself about."

This with a very quick motion.

"Put your left hand in, Put your left hand out,
Shake your left a little, And turn yourselves about."

Then we sung and danced Luby in chorus. Our spectators the fathers, mothers, and grandmothers and aunts found the performance very amusing indeed, and laughed till they cried at the odd manoevers and singing. After the hands the feet were exercised in the same way. The children were beginning to perform with great zest, being delighted to make so much sport for their grave elders. After the feet had been duly exercised, we bowed the head.

"Put your ugly mug in."

This was the funniest of all. Herberts large black eyes were sparkling with delight, and every fibre seemed to dance.

"There will be no sleep for him tonight," said his father, sadly, after the company had left, but he never slept more soundly. The cure was found. A lively play before retiring helped him to a good night's rest.

Occasionally they practised a few calisthenics the older ones had learned at school, but games were the favorite recreation. I taught them all the old plays I ever knew, and that was a great many. Going to Jerusalem, Stage coach, Tucker, Apple sauce, The Crowing Hen, etc., that we used to play when we were children. I need not describe them to you. For the older ones we had the Horn game, Pantomimic Charades, Throwing Light, Positives and Comparitives, the Plant game, Conundrums, Rhymes, Puzzles, Anagrams, etc.

You know some of my friends thought the time and money I had spent in college thrown away, because I married so soon, but nearly every thing I learned was called into requisition in bringing up our family. I taught every thing, from Mental Arithmetic to Conic Sections. None of the children went away to school; they attended the best schools in our vicinity and studied at home. The languages I had learned came in use, and I studied Spanish with Herbert to help him along. Indeed I had little chance to forget any thing with all those eager questioners around me. No one needs a broader and fuller education than the mother.

"Every thing I know that is worth knowing, mamma taught me," I heard George say one day.

"She did not teach me to play the violin," said Herbert.

I did not wish the children to forget their mother, yet for a long time, any mention of her brought sadness and weeping. They spoke of her as dead, and buried in the grave. It seemed hard to make them understand that only her body was in the grave, that she was living; was born into a higher life; that she had a new home and was living a happy and beautiful life, and did not forget them, but loved them just as tenderly as when she lived here with them. Gradually the old dark shadows passed from their minds, and they came to feel that it was selfish to grieve for her; that love for her would make them try to do what would please her and they cherished only sweet and tender memories of their mother.

Now this interesting family scattered far and wide, cherish only tender and pleasant memories of their step-mother, Cousin Esther, who has crossed the great river, and whose ministries were abundantly blessed in many ways. The path of duty was to her the royal road to blessedness.

Classroom Etiquette

The following are the requisites for successful management in the schoolroom:

The teacher must be a good judge of human nature. If so, his knowledge will teach him that no two children are born with precisely the same organization. This difference in mentality will make one child a natural linguist, another will naturally excel in mathematics, another will exhibit a fondness for drawing, and another for philosophy. Understanding and observing this, he will, without anger or impatience, assist the backward student, and will direct the more forward, ever addressing each child in the most respectful manner.

As few rules as possible should be made, and the object and necessity for the rule should be fully explained to the school by the teacher. When a rule has been made obedience to it should be enforced. Firmness, united with gentleness, is one of the most important qualifications which a teacher can possess.

Everything should be in order and the exercises of the day should be carried forward according to an arranged programme. The rooms should be swept, the fires built and the first and second bells rung with exact punctuality. In the same manner each recitation should come at an appointed time throughout the school hours.

The programme of exercises should be so varied as to give each pupil a variety of bodily and mental exercise. Thus, music, recreation, study, recitation, declamation, etc., should be so varied as to develop all the child's powers. Not only should boys and girls store their minds with knowledge, but they should be trained in the best methods of writing and speaking, whereby they may be able to impart the knowledge which they possess.

The teacher should require the strictest order and neatness upon the part of all the students. Clean hands, clean face and neatly combed hair should characterize every pupil, while a mat in the doorway should remind every boy and girl of the necessity of entering the schoolroom with clean hands and shoes. Habits of neatness and order thus formed will go with the pupils through life.

At least a portion of each day should be set apart by the teacher in which to impart to the pupils a knowledge of etiquette. Students should be trained to enter the room quietly, to always close without noise the door through which they pass, to make introductions gracefully, to bow with ease and dignity, to shake hands properly, to address others courteously, to make a polite reply when spoken to, to sit and stand gracefully, to do the right thing in the right place, and thus, upon all occasions, to appear to advantage.

All the furnishings of the schoolroom should be such as to inspire the holiest, loftiest, and noblest ambition in the child. A schoolroom should be handsomely decorated. The aquarium, the trailing vine, the blossom and the specimens of natural history should adorn the teacher's desk and the windows, while handsome pictures should embellish the walls. In short, the pupils should be surrounded with such an array of beauty as will constantly inspire them to higher and nobler achievements.

Boys and girls should be taught that which they will use when they become men and women. In the first place they will talk more than they will do anything else. By every means possible they should be trained to be correct, easy, fluent and pleasant speakers; and next to this they should be trained to be ready writers. To be this, they should be schooled in penmanship, punctuation, capitilization, composition and the writing of every description of forms, from the note of invitation to an agreement, from the epistle to a friend to the promissary note, from the letter of introduction to the report of a meeting.

Above all, the teacher should be thoroughly imbued with the importance of inculcating in the mind of the student a knowledge of general principles. Thus, in the study of geography, the pupil should be taught that the earth is spherical in form; that its outer surface is divided into land and water; that the land is divided into certain grand sections, peopled with different races of human beings who exhibit special characteristics. That civilization is the result of certain causes, and progress in the human race arises from the inevitable law of nature that everything goes from the lower steadily toward the higher. A study of the causes which make difference in climate, difference in animals, difference in intellectual and moral developments among the races—a general study of causes thus will make such an impression upon the child's mind as will never be effaced; while the simple study of facts such as load the mind with names of bays, islands, rivers, etc., is the crowding of the memory with that which is likely in time to be nearly all forgotten.

Thus, in the study of history, dates will be forgotten, while the outlines of the rise and fall of kingdoms, and the causes which produced the same, if rightly impressed by the teacher, will be ever stored in the mind of the pupil.

So should the teacher instruct the student in every branch of study, remembering that facts are liable to be forgotten, but fundamental principles and causes, well understood, will be forever remembered.

It is of the utmost importance, also, that the teacher continuously and persistently keep before the student the importance of temperance, justice and truth; as, without them, however superior the education, the individual is entirely without balance, and is always liable to fall. The teacher should never relax his efforts in this direction.

The good teacher will be a living example in all he teaches to others. If wise, he will seldom or never resort to the infliction of corporal pain on the pupil, although, if a law or rule be violated, it is of the utmost importance that a just punishment follow the violation, but this should never be such as will destroy the child's self-respect.

Duty of the Pupil

It should be the aim of the student to be punctual in attendance at school, to be thorough in study, and good in recitation. The boy or girl who would be successful in after-life must lay the foundation of success in youth. They should fully understand the importance of improving their school days for this purpose.

The student who seeks every opportunity to idle away his time in making sport and amusement for himself and fellow students will live to regret that he thus wasted his time. The happy, sportive, joyous, laughing boy and girl shed happiness wherever they go if they are careful to control their gayety and allow its flow only in the proper place; but they should never permit the love of the mirthful to infringe on the rules of the schoolroom or the laws of etiquette. On the contrary, true courtesy should teach them to use every endeavor to aid the teacher in his work, as in so doing they are themselves reaping the benefits.

The boy and girl at school foretell the future man and woman. Those who are prompt, punctual and orderly will be so in after-life. Those who are truthful, reliable and honest in childhood, will be trusted in position and place in after-years; and those who store the mind in youth with valuable knowledge will possess that which can never be lost, but on the contrary will always be a means by which they may procure a livelihood; and, if united with energy and perserverance, will be sure to give them reputation, eminence of position, and wealth.

The boy should never take pride in disobedience to the rules of school. To be a truant, to be indolent, to be working mischief, evinces no talent; any rowdy could do this; most worthless men

did this when they attended school. It requires effort to be a good scholar; it evinces brain-power to be a good student.

The youth should earnestly resolve to achieve an honorable and noble position in life. With the wide opportunities which open to the ambitions and the enterprising in this age of progression there is no limit to the greatness which the thoroughly earnest student may attain. The idle and dissolute will, naturally, of their own weight drop out by the wayside and sink from sight. The plodder who is content to go the dull, daily round in the same narrow rut will get the reward of his labor, though he never betters his condition. But the earnest, original, aspiring, energetic, intelligent worker can always be sure of new fields to enter, nobler victories to gain, and grander work to be accomplished.

Out and About

TWO STORES CONTRASTED.

THE above shows the interior of the grocery store where cheese, butter, flour, sugar and other articles, containing moisture, are saturated with tobacco smoke. It may be the privilege of the proprietor to make his store the general resort of amusement seekers, loungers and smokers, but such a course is never to be commended as profitable to business.

THE charming window display of goods in this store attract to the interior, where the order and general neatness are evidences that the groceries for sale here are of pure quality, the butter not filled with the flavor of tobacco, nor the sugar with kerosene. These pleasant surroundings further indicate that prompt and genteel attention will be given the customer.

Etiquette of Shopping

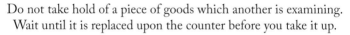

Purchasers should, as far as possible, patronize the merchants of their own town. It is poor policy to send money abroad for articles which can be bought as cheaply at home.

Do not take hold of a piece of goods which another is examining. Wait until it is replaced upon the counter before you take it up.

Injuring goods when handling, pushing aside other persons, hanging upon the counter, whispering, loud talk and laughter, when in a store, are all evidence of ill-breeding.

Never attempt to "beat down" prices when shopping. If the price does not suit, go elsewhere. The just and upright merchant will have but one price for his goods, and he will strictly adhere to it.

It is an insult to a clerk or merchant to suggest to a customer about to purchase that may buy cheaper or better elsewhere. It is also rude to give your opinion, unasked, about the goods that another is purchasing.

Never expect a clerk to leave another customer to wait on you; and, when attending upon you, do not cause him to wait while you visit with another. When the purchases are made let them be sent to your home, and thus avoid loading yourself with bundles.

Treat clerks, when shopping, respectfully, and give them no more trouble than is necessary. Ask for what is wanted, explicitly, and if you wish to make examination with a view to future purchase, say so. Be perfectly frank. There is no necessity in practicing deceit.

The rule should be to pay for goods when you buy them. If, however, you are trusted by the merchant, you should be very particular to pay your indebtedness when you agree to. By doing as you promise, you acquire good habits of promptitude, and at the same time establish credit and make reputation among those with whom you deal.

It is rude in the extreme to find fault and to make sneering remarks about goods. To draw unfavorable comparisons between the goods and those found at other stores does no good, and shows want of deference and respect to those who are waiting on you. Politely state that the goods are not what you want, and, while you may buy, you prefer to look further.

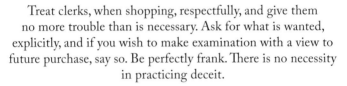

Etiquette of the Street: Rules of Conduct to be Observed

A gentleman walking with a lady should accommodate his step and pace to hers. For the gentleman to be some distance ahead, presents a bad appearance.

Should protection on the street be necessary, it is customary for the gentleman to give his right arm to the lady; but if more convenient, he may give the left.

It is courtesy to give silent, respectful attention as a funeral procession passes. It shows want of respect to pass between the carriages while the procession is moving.

Staring at people, spitting, looking back after they pass, saluting people across the street, calling out loudly or laughing at people as they go by, are all evidences of ill-breeding.

The gentleman accompanying a lady should hold the door open for the lady to enter first. Should he be near the door when a lady, unattended, is about to enter, he will do the same for her.

In the evening, or whenever safety may require, a gentleman should give a lady his arm. It is not customary in other cases to do so on the street, unless with an elderly lady, or the couple be husband and wife.

A gentleman will assist a lady over a bad crossing, or from an omnibus or carriage, without waiting for the formality of an introduction. When the service is performed, he will raise his hat, bow, and pass on.

In the street car or an omnibus, the passengers who are seated should strive to give seats to those who are standing, rendering such accomodation as they would themselves desire under similar circumstances.

When crossing the pavement, the lady should raise her dress with the right hand, a little above the ankle. To raise the dress with both hands, is vulgar, and can be excused only when the mud is very deep.

No gentleman will smoke when walking with, or standing in the presence of, a lady in the street. He should remove the cigar from her presence entirely, even though permission be granted to continue the smoking.

A gentleman should give his seat to any lady who may be standing in a public conveyance. For this favor she should thank him, which courtesy he should acknowledge by a slight bow. In an omnibus he will pass up the ladies' fares.

A true lady will go quietly and unobtrusively about her business when on the street, never seeking to atract the attention of the opposite sex, at the same time recognizing acquaintances with a courteous bow, and friends with pleasant words of greeting.

Swinging the arms when walking, eating upon the street, sucking the parasol handles, pushing violently through a crowd, very loud and boisterous talking and laughing on the streets, and whispering in public conveyances, are all evidences of ill-breeding in ladies.

A lady should have the escort of a gentleman in the evening. A gentleman at the house where she may call may return with her if she goes unattended; gossip and scandal are best avoided, however, if she have some one from her home call for her at an appointed hour.

On the narrow street-crossing the gentleman will allow the lady to precede him, that he may see that no injury befalls her.

Should a lady stop in the street, when meeting a gentleman, it is courtesy for him to stop also. Should his business be urgent, he will apologize for not continuing the conversation, and ask to be excused. Should it be desirable to lengthen the interview, and the lady resumes her walk in the midst of the conversation, it is courtesy for him to turn and accompany her. Should she desire to end the conversation, a slight bow from her will indicate the fact, when he should bid her "good day" and take his leave.

Chatterbox Corner

DINNER IN THE SUBURBS

THE SACRED HOUR IN WHICH YOUR FRIENDS KNOW THEY CAN REACH YOU BY TELEPHONE. AN IDEA
TO SAVE GETTING UP FROM THE TABLE

Modern Improvements

By "Aunt Ruth" Belle C. Greene[9]

(fiction)

I must tell ye how Deacon Jones got fooled, when I was to his house last summer. You know the deacon's awful savin', and he hadn't took no newspaper for years; said how he could hear enough o' the wicked doin's of the world without payin' money to read about 'em.

---

[9]   The name appearing in the book is almost certainly an alias. The actual author's identity is unknown.

Wall, he went over to Bangton one mornin' to carry some butter and eggs, and buy groceries, and one thing n'other they was needin', and Mis' Jones and me we had a good long day all to ourselves.

Between sundown and dark, we was settin' together knittin' and talkin', when the deacon come in. He laid his bundles down on the table without sayin' a word. He alwers invariable used to say, "There, wife, there's your groceries; use 'em sparin', use 'em sparin'." So this time we didn't know what to make on him. He looked uncommon sober, too.

"Father," says Mis' Jones, "what's the matter? Didn't the things sell well?"

"Yes, the things sold well enough," says he, "but I found out somethin' down to Bangton that's just about upset me."

"The bank haint failed—"

"No, no! For the land sake, aint there no troubles in this world but *money* trouble!" says the deacon real snappish.

"Why, yes, of course," says Mis' Jones, "but dew tell us what *is the matter*!"

Then he set down and told us. "You know Widder Grimes' oldest boy, James, has been to work in Barker's grocery store for more'n a year. You remember what a nice boy he's alwers been,— good habits and all that,—and sence his father died he's the main stay o' the family, as you might say. It was only the other day his mother was tellin' me about him; how well he was gettin' along, and how Barker meant to take him in pardner this fall. She seemed so proud and happy over it. She's jest bound up in that boy! But I'll tell ye how it was. After I'd done my arrants and packed all the bundles away under the buggy seat, I went back into Barker's store and set down on a box to eat a bite o' lunch and rest me a minnit, when James Grimes come in. I noticed he looked kinder queer. He steered straight for the back end o' the store, and lea-nin' up agin the wall, begun to go through with the silliest lot o' performances I ever see. If he hadn't been more'n six year old, I should a thought he was makin' believe at some kind o' child's play! He pertended to be talkin' to somebody, hollered "hullo!" and "all right!" and a whole mess o' stuff, then laughed as hearty as could be, at his own nonsense. I couldn't believe it of James and I turns to Jeff Adams, standin' by me, "Drunk, ain't he?" says I. Jeff didn't make no answer, only winked one eye and grinned. It was a good joke to him I s'pose, but it wa'n't to me; I tell you I felt like death, and I went and got out my team and come away as quick's I could. And the wust on't is, it'll just about kill the Widder Grimes!"

Mis' Jones wiped her eyes, "Poor woman, God help her!" says she.

All of a suddin an idee popped into my head. I says to the deacon:

"Did James say 'Hullo!' when he fust begun to talk?"[10]

"Yes. He kep' sayin' on't over'n and over."

"And didn't he hold somethin' up to his ear?"

"I didn't mind. There was a lot o' things all cluttered up hangin' on the wall behind him; corn poppers, and tin-ware, and so on—but why, what are you drivin' at, Ruth Ann?"

"Wall," says I, "I think James was jest talkin' through a tel-efone—one o' them talkin' machines, you know."

---

[10] The expression "Hollo!" or "Holla!" was originally used to indicate surprise or call attention to something. When the telephone started to become popular, people considered its jangling noise so unnerving that "Hello" became the standard telephonic greeting.

"*Telefone!*" says the deacon, all struck of a heap. "I've heerd on 'em. Do you s'pose they've got one in Barker's store? I dunno."

"How *should* ye know *anything*, for that matter, when we don't take no newspaper!" said his wife, kinder spiteful.

"I swanny!" says the deacon, "if I don't believe you're right, Ruth Ann! James *wouldn't* git drunk—I might a knowed it!"

He went off post haste over to neighbor Fuller's to make inquiries, and he found out that Barker *had* got a telefone, and that James Grimes was stiddy as an eight-day clock, jest as he alwers had been.

The best on't was, the deacon concluded to take a newspaper.

Etiquette of Conversation

Use clear, distinct words to express your ideas, although the tone of your voice should be subdued.

Be cool, collected and self-possessed, using respectful, chaste, and appropriate language.

Always defend the absent person who is being spoken of, as far as truth and justice will permit.

Allow people that you are with to do their full share of the talking if they evince a willingness to converse.

Beware of talking much about yourself. Your merits will be discovered in due time without the necessity of sounding your own praises.

Show the courtesy, when another person joins the group where you are relating an incident, of recapitulating what has been said, for the advantage of the new-comer.

Recollect that the object of conversation is to entertain and amuse; the social gathering, therefore, should not be made the arena of dispute. Even slight mistakes and inaccuracies it is well to overlook, rather than to allow inharmony to present itself.

Aim to adapt your conversation to the comprehension of those with whom you are conversing. Be careful that you do not undervalue them. It is possible that they are as intelligent as yourself, and their conversation can, perhaps, take as wide a range as your own.

Remember that the person to whom you are speaking is not to blame for the opinion he entertains. Opinions are not made *by* us, but they are made *for* us by circumstances. With the same organization, training and circumstances around us, we would have the same opinions ourselves.

Remember that people are fond of talking of their own affairs. The mother likes to talk of her children, the mechanic of his workmanship, the laborer of what he can accomplish. Give every one an opportunity, and you will gain much valuable information besides being thought courteous and well-bred.

Be patient. The foreigner cannot, perhaps, recall the word he desires; the speaker may be slow of speech; you may have heard the story a dozen times; but even then you must evince interest and listen patiently through. By so doing you gain the esteem of the person with whom you are conversing.

What to Avoid in Social Conversation

Do not manifest impatience.

Do not engage in argument.

Do not interrupt another when speaking.

Do not find fault, although you may gently criticise.

Do not talk of your private, personal and family matters.

Do not appear to notice inacurries [sic] of speech in others.

Do not allow yourself to lose temper or to speak excitedly.

True Ladies and Proper Gentlemen

Do not allude to unfortunate peculiarities of any one present.

Do not always commence a conversation by allusion to the weather.

Do not, when narrating an incident, continually say "you see," "you know," etc.

Do not introduce professional or other topics in which the company generally cannot take an interest.

Do not talk very loud. A firm, clear, distinct, yet mild, gentle and musical voice has great power.

Do not be absent-minded, requiring the speaker to repeat what has been said that you may understand.

Do not speak disrespectfully of personal appearance when any one present may have the same defects.

Do not try to force yourself into the confidence of others. If they give their confidence, never betray it.

Do not use profanity, vulgar terms, slang phrases, words of double meaning, or language that will bring the blush to any person.

Do not intersperse your language with foreign words and high-sounding terms. It shows affectation, and will draw ridicule upon you.

Do not carry on a conversation with another in company about matters of which the general company knows nothing. It is almost as impolite as to whisper.

Do not allow yourself to speak ill of the absent if it can be avoided; the day may come when some friend will be needed to defend you in your absence.

Do not speak with contempt and ridicule of a locality where you may be visiting. Find something to truthfully praise and commend; thus make yourself agreeable.

True Ladies and Proper Gentlemen

Do not make a pretense of gentility, nor parade the fact that you are a descendant of any notable family. You must pass for just what you are, and must stand on your own merit.

Do not contradict. In making a correction say, "I beg your pardon, but I had an impression that it was so and so." Be careful in correcting, as you may be wrong yourself.

Do not be unduly familiar; you will merit contempt if you are. Neither should you be dogmatic in your assertions, arrogating to yourself much consequence in your opinions.
Do not be too lavish in your praise of various members of your own family when speaking to strangers; the person to whom you are speaking may know some faults that you do not.

Do not allow yourself to use personal abuse when speaking to another, as in so doing you may make that person a life-long enemy. A few kind, courteous words might have made him a life-long friend.

Do not discuss politics or religion in general company. You probably would not convert your opponent, and he will not convert you. To discuss those topics is to arouse feeling without any good result.

Do not make a parade of being acquainted with distinguished or wealthy people, of having been to college, or of having visited foreign lands. All this is no evidence of any real genuine worth on your part.

Do not use the surname alone when speaking of your husband or wife to others. To say to another, that "I told Jones," referring to your husband, sounds badly. Whereas to say, "I told Mr. Jones," shows respect and good-breeding.

Do not feel it incumbent upon yourself to carry your point in conversation. Should the person with whom you are conversing feel the same, your talk will lead into violent argument.

Do not yield to bashfulness. Do not isolate yourself, sitting back in a corner, waiting for someone to come and talk with you. Step out; have something to say. Though you may not say it very well, keep on. You will gain courage and will improve. It is as much your duty to entertain others as theirs to amuse you.

Do not attempt to pry into the private affairs of others by asking what their profits are, what things cost, whether Melissa ever had a beau, and why Amarette never got married. All such questions are extremely impertinent, and are likely to meet with rebuke.

Do not whisper in company; do not engage in private conversation; do not speak a foreign language which the general company present may not comprehend, unless it is understood that the foreigner is unable to speak your own language.

Do not take it upon yourself to admonish comparative strangers on religious topics; the persons to whom you speak may have decided convictions of their own in opposition to yours, and your over-zeal may seem to them an impertinence.

Do not aspire to be a great story-teller; an inveterate teller of long stories becomes very tiresome. To tell one or two witty, short, new stories, appropriate to the occasion, is about all that one person should inflict on the company.

Do not indulge in satire; no doubt you are witty, and you could say a most cutting thing that would bring the laugh of the company upon your opponent, but you must not allow it, unless to rebuke an impertinent fellow who can be suppressed no other way.

Do not spend your time in talking scandal; you sink your own moral nature by so doing, and you are, perhaps, doing great injustice to those about whom you talk. You probably do not understand all the circumstances. Were they understood, you would, doubtless, be much more lenient.

Do not flatter; in doing so you embarrass those upon whom you bestow praise, as they may not wish to offend you by repelling it, and yet they realize that if they accept it they merit your contempt. You may, however, commend their work whenever it can truthfully be done; but do not bestow praise where it is not deserved.

Paying Calls

At Other People's Convenience:
"A Whole Week Put Out of Joint
for a Twenty Minutes' Call"

"By the way, Judith," said Julius, one Monday evening at the tea-table, "I met Mr. Dominie in the post-office this afternoon, and he said that he and Mrs. Dominie had intended to come out to see us this forenoon, but they found, at the last minute, that the Deacon was intending to use his horse himself."

"Bless that dear old deacon," said I, fervently. "I owe him one."

"Yes, it *was* luck!" said Julius.

"I should think so! How any couple, in their senses, could ever think of making a surprise visit on Monday morning, I don't see! What did you tell him?"

"Well, you see, I didn't like to remind him it was washing day—they have kept house, and know all about it, and they know we are doing our own work, for he asked how it agreed with you in this weather, and when we expected 'Mandy back—so I just told him that they must not be discouraged, but must try again."

"And what did he say to that?"

"Why, he said they meant to try it again to-morrow."

"To-morrow! and all the ironing to do, and nothing fresh baked!"

"Yes, I knew it wouldn't suit, but what could I do?"

"Nothing, of course. We will have to make the best of it. I will put off the ironing, and do some baking instead—bright and early before they get here."

So the next morning I got up betimes, set the whole house in spotless order, baked rolls and cake, got a chicken pie under way and made a salad. Then I dressed myself in a white muslin, with ruffled apron, and gathered fresh flowers for all of the vases. Then I sat down and hulled a bowlful of ripe, dewy strawberries, which Julius had gathered for me. Mr. and Mrs. Dominie boarded in the village, and would, I knew, appreciate our delicious country fare. He was preaching for us for six months "on trial." They were an elderly couple, whose children were all scattered, and were fond of visiting. We did not feel very well acquainted with them, and wished to do them honor. At 11 o'clock Julius came in from the garden, to make himself presentable. He found me putting the last touches to the dinner-table, so that only the hot food would have to be added at "dishing up" time.

"Haven't come yet!" he exclaimed.

"No," I said; "they seem inclined to be very fashionable. One would think the cool of the morning much pleasanter for driving this time of year.

"Yes indeed; but they may be along any minute now."

A quarter past—half past—three-quarters—12. Still no minister, nor minister's wife. Julius paced between the front veranda and the gate, while I busied myself trying to keep the dinner hot, without drying it to chips. One o'clock struck; then Julius came in, saying: "We might as well give them up and have dinner. Something must have happened to detain them, and perhaps they will come this afternoon."

So we ate hurriedly, and Julius helped me to set all to rights; then, tired out, I sat down, with a new magazine and a basket of mending. At four o'clock, there still being no sign of our visitors, Julius came in and said: "It's time to go to the post-office; the mail must surely be in. Perhaps I'll meet Mr. Dominie, or some one from the Deacon's, and find out what the trouble is."

When he returned, he said, in answer to my eager inquiries: "Yes; I met Mr. Dominie himself, the first one, and he said they did think of coming this morning, but Mrs. Dominie thought it looked like rain."

"Like rain! Why, I never heard of such nonsense. It has been a lovely day!"

"So *I* thought; but of course I couldn't contradict him. Then he said, if it was pleasant, they would come to-morrow."

I groaned: "Then I must put off the ironing again."

So the next morning I again busied myself preparing good things for dinner and making the house as attractive as possible.

When Julius and I a second time sat down to our belated dinner alone, I was fairly boiling with indignation.

"Do you know what I think of Mr. Dominie?" I exclaimed. "I think he is a first-class fraud!"

"I wouldn't say that," said Julius. "He may have had some good reason this time. Perhaps someone was taken sick and sent for him."

"Then she ought to have sent us word. It is shameful for them to be so rude!"

"So it is; and it has made you so much extra work, too."

"Yes, I have worked twice as hard as usual; and here, the week is half gone, and not a piece ironed."

When Julius came home that evening he said: "I saw Mr. Dominie, and he said he was sorry they didn't get out this morning, but Mrs. Dominie thought she felt one of her attacks of headache coming on, so he thought they'd better postpone it; but they will surely be out to-morrow."

"Indeed!" said I, then added, viciously, "I hope it will rain pitchforks!"

"Oh well, they'll *come* this time, and then it will be over, and we won't ask them again."

"They don't wait to be asked," I said, "but seem to think their visits are such treats to us that they may put us to any amount of trouble, and it's all right."

Well, the whole programme was again repeated, and still our visitors did not appear. It was fair all day until late afternoon, then a thunder-shower came up, preventing Julius from going after the mail, so we did not learn what trifle prevented their coming this time. At the tea-table I said, "Well, to-morrow is Friday, and, minister or no minister, I am going to iron."

So, the next morning, I went to work on my belated ironing, in fear and trembling, starting at every sound, until I became so nervous I felt like flying—for fear they would come and catch me unawares in the short-sleeved Mother Hubbard I always wore when ironing. The day waned, but they did not come. When Julius started to the village, I took a book and threw myself into the hammock, completely tired out. He had been gone some time, when I heard voices. Looking out, there were Mr. and Mrs. Dominie coming up the front path. I met them at the door and tried to be cordial, but felt that it was a hollow mockery. It was impossible to keep the reproach out of my voice when I spoke of having expected them to dinner each day since Monday.

"Yes, we were *so* disappointed," said Mrs. Dominie; "but every time we planned to come, something would happen to prevent."

I think they expected an invitation to tea, but I forgot (?) it, and said, moreover, nothing about future visits. I suppose it was not very polite, but "the worm will turn."

Julius laughed rather grimly, when he came home and heard about the visit. "A whole week put out of joint for a 20-minutes' call," he said.

"Yes," said I; "and if Mr. Dominie remains here after his six months are up, it won't be my fault. A man who has so little regard for his own word, and other people's convenience, is a public nuisance!"

"Amen," said Julius.

The Inquisitive, Disagreeable Caller.

AMONG the disagreeable callers are the husband and wife who come with a child and a small dog; the husband making himself familiar with the hostess, the dog barking at the cat, the child taking the free run of the house, while the wife, in the meantime, passes around the room, handling and examining the ornaments.

Other unpleasant callers are the man with the muddy boots, and the individual just in out of the rain, from whose overcoat and umbrella the water drips on the carpet.

Ready to Go, Yet Waiting.

SOME evening callers make themselves odious by continuing their visit too long, and even when they have risen to depart they lack decision of purpose to go, but will frequently stand several minutes before taking final leave, and then when wraps are on and they are nearly gone, they will stand in the doorway to tell one more story while the hostess protects herself as best she can from the incoming gusts of wind and storm, sometimes thus taking a cold that ends in death. When the guest is ready to go—*go.*

Etiquette of Calling

The morning call should be very brief. This formal call is mainly one of ceremony, and from ten to twenty minutes is a sufficient length of time to prolong it. It should never exceed half an hour.

In making a formal call, a lady does not remove her bonnet or wraps.

Unless there be a certain evening set apart for receiving, the formal call should be made in the morning.

It is customary, according to the code of etiquette, to call all the hours of daylight morning, and after nightfall evening.

Calls may be made in the morning or the evening. The call in the morning should not be made before 12M.[11], nor later than 5 p.m.

---

[11] Meridian—i.e., noon.

A gentleman, making a formal call in the morning, must retain his hat in his hand. He may leave umbrella and cane in the hall, but not his hat and gloves. The act of retaining hat indicates a formal call.[12]

When a gentleman accompanies a lady at a morning call (which is seldom), he assists her up the steps, rings the bell, and follows her into the reception room. It is for the lady to determine when they should leave.[13]

All uncouth and ungraceful positions are especially unbecoming among ladies and gentlemen in the parlor. Thus, standing with the arms akimbo, sitting astride a chair, [a man] wearing the hat, and smoking in the presence of ladies, leaning back in the chair, standing with legs crossed and feet on the chairs—all those evince lack of polished manners.

---

[12]   The umbrella will drip and the cane may knock things over. Leaving everything in the hall, however, gives the disconcerting impression you mean to stay indefinitely.

[13]   These calls were a vital form of social networking to the Victorians—and the practice of them was dominated by the women. Men were expected to keep themselves in their offices except on very specific occasions.

If possible, avoid calling at the lunch or dinner hour. Among society people the most fashionable hours for calling are from 12 M. to 3 P.M. At homes where dinner or lunch is taken at noon, calls may be made from 2 to 5 P.M.

Should other callers be announced, it is well, as soon as the bustle attending the new arrival is over, to arise quietly, take leave of the hostess, bow to the visitors, and retire, without apparently doing so because of the new arrivals. This saves the hostess the trouble of entertaining two sets of callers.

To say bright and witty things during the call of ceremony, and go so soon that the hostess will desire the caller to come again, is much more the pleasant. No topic of a political or religious character should be admitted to the conversation, nor any subject of absorbing interest likely to lead to discussion.[14]

A lady engaged upon fancy sewing of any kind, or needlework, need not necessarily lay aside the same during the call of intimate acquaintance. Conversation can flow just as freely while the visit continues. During visits of ceremony, however, strict attention should be given to entertaining the callers.

---

[14] The idea here is to get in and out quickly!

Gentlemen may make morning calls on the following occasions: To convey congratulations or sympathy and condolence, to meet a friend who has just returned from abroad, to inquire after the health of a lady who may have accepted his escort the previous day. (He should not delay the matter more than a day.) He may call upon those to whom letters of introduction are given, to express thanks for any favor which may have been rendered him, or to return a call. A great variety of circumstances will also determine when at other times he should make calls.

What Should Be Avoided When Calling

Do not stare around the room.

Do not take a dog or small child.

Do not linger at the dinner-hour.

Do not lay aside the bonnet at a formal call.

Do not fidget with your cane, hat or parasol.

Do not make a call of ceremony on a wet day.

Do not turn your back to one seated near you.

Do not touch the piano, unless invited to do so.

Do not handle ornaments or furniture in the room.

Do not make a display of consulting your watch.

Do not go to the room of an invalid, unless invited.

Do not remove the gloves when making a formal call.

Do not continue the call longer when conversation begins to lag.

Do not remain when you find the lady on the point of going out.

True Ladies and Proper Gentlemen

Do not make the first call if you are a new-comer in the neighborhood.

Do not open or shut doors or windows or alter the arrangement of the room.

Do not enter a room without first knocking and receiving an invitation to come in.

Do not resume your seat after having risen to go, unless for important reasons.

Do not walk around the room, examining pictures, while waiting for the hostess.

Do not introduce politics, religion or weighty topics for conversation when making calls.

Do not prolong the call if the room is crowded. It is better to call a day or two afterwards.

Do not call upon a person in reduced circumstance with a display of wealth, dress and equipage.

Do not tattle. Do not speak ill of your neighbors. Do not carry gossip from one family to another.

Do not, if a gentleman, seat yourself upon the sofa beside the hostess, or in near proximity, unless invited to do so.

Do not, if a lady, call upon a gentleman, except officially or professionally, unless he may be a confirmed invalid.

Do not take a strange gentleman with you, unless positively certain that his introduction will be received with favor.

Do not, if a gentleman, leave the hat in the hall when making a formal call. If the call is extended into a visit, it may be set aside. Whether sitting or standing, the hat may be gracefully held in the hand.

Fig. 6. UNGRACEFUL POSITIONS.

No. **1.** Stands with arms akimbo.

" **2.** Sits with elbows on the knees.

" **3.** Sits astride the chair, and wears his hat in the parlor.

" **4.** Stains the wall paper by pressing against it with his hand; eats an apple alone, and stands with his legs crossed.

No. 5. Rests his foot upon the chair cushion.

" 6. Tips back his chair, soils the wall by resting his head against it, and smokes in the presence of ladies.

FIG. 7. GENTILITY IN THE PARLOR.

The figures in the above illustra-
a represent graceful postures to
assumed by both ladies and gen-
nen in the parlor. As will be
n, whether holding hat or fan,
er sitting or standing, the posi-
s are all easy and graceful.

To assume an easy genteel atti-
tude, the individual must be self-
possessed. To be so, attention must
be given to easy flow of language,
happy expression of thought, study
of cultured society and the general
laws of etiquette.

Etiquette of the Table

Rules to be Observed

Sit upright, neither too close nor too far away from the table.

Open and spread upon your lap or breast a napkin, if one is provided—otherwise a handkerchief.

Do not be in haste; compose yourself; put your mind into a pleasant condition, and resolve to eat slowly.

Keep the hands from the table until your time comes to be served. It is rude to take knife and fork in hand and commence drumming on the table while you are waiting.

Taking ample time in eating will give you better health, greater wealth, longer life and more happiness. These are what we may obtain by eating slowly in a pleasant frame of mind, thoroughly masticating the food.

FIG. 11. BAD MANNERS AT THE TABLE.

No. 1. Tips back his chair.
" 2. Eats with his mouth too full.
" 3. Feeds a dog at the table.
" 4. Holds his knife improperly.
" 5. Engages in violent argument at the meal-time.
" 6. Lounges upon the table.
" 7. Brings a cross child to the table.

No. 8. Drinks from the saucer, and laps with his tongue the last drop from the plate.
" 9. Comes to the table in his shirt-sleeves, and puts his feet beside his chair.
" 10. Picks his teeth with his fingers.
" 11. Scratches her head and is frequently unnecessarily getting up from the table.

Errors to be Avoided

Do not speak disrespectfully to the waiters, nor apologize to them for making them trouble; it is their business to bring forward the food called for. It is courtesy, however, when asked if you desire a certain article, to reply, "If you please;" "Not any, I thank you," etc.; when calling for an article, to say, "Will you please bring me," etc.; and when the article has been furnished to say, "Thank you."

Never eat very fast.

Never fill the mouth very full.

Never open your mouth when chewing.

Never make noise with the mouth or throat.

Never attempt to talk with the mouth full.

Never attempt to leave the table with food in the mouth.

True Ladies and Proper Gentlemen

Never soil the table-cloth if it is possible to avoid it.

Never carry away fruits and confectionary from the table.

Never encourage a dog or cat to play with you at the table.

Never use anything but a fork or spoon in feeding yourself.

Never explain at the table why certain foods do not agree with you.

Never introduce disgusting or unpleasant topics for conversation.

Never pick your teeth or put your hand in your mouth while eating.

Never cut bread; always break it, spreading with butter each piece as you eat it.

Never come to the table in your shirt sleeves, with dirty hands or disheveled hair.

Never express a choice for any particular parts of a dish, unless requested to do so.

Never hesitate to take the last piece of bread or the last cake; there are probably more.

Never call loudly for the waiter, nor attract attention to yourself by boisterous conduct.

Never hold bones in your fingers while you eat from them. Cut the meat with a knife.

Never use your own knife when cutting butter. Always use a knife assigned to that purpose.

Never pare an apple, peach, or pear for another at the table without holding it with a fork.

True Ladies and Proper Gentlemen

Never wipe your fingers on the table-cloth, nor clean them in your mouth. Use the napkin.

Never allow butter, soup or other food to remain on your whiskers. Use the napkin frequently.

Never wear gloves at the table, unless the hands from some special reason are unfit to be seen.

Never, when serving others, overload the plate nor force upon them delicacies which they decline.

Never pour sauce over meat and vegetables when helping others. Place it at one side, on the plate.

Never make a display of finding fault with your food. Very quietly have it changed if you want it different.

Never pass your plate with knife and fork on the same. Remove them, and allow them to rest upon a piece of bread.

Never make a display when removing hair, insects or other disagreeable things from your food. Place them quietly under the edge of your plate.

Never make an effort to clean your plate or the bones you have been eating from too clean; it looks as if you left off hungry.

Never tip back in your chair nor lounge upon the table; neither assume any position that is awkward or ill-bred.

Never, at one's own table or at a dinner-party elsewhere, leave before the rest have finished without asking to be excused. At a hotel or boarding house this rule need not be observed.

Never feel obliged to cut off the kernels with a knife when eating green corn[15]; eaten from the cob, the corn is much the sweetest.

---

[15] "Green corn" signifies fresh corn—as opposed to the kind which is ground into meal.

Never eat so much of any one article so as to attract attention, as some people do who eat large quantities of butter, sweet cake, cheese or other articles.

Never expectorate at the table; also avoid sneezing or coughing. It is better to arise quietly from the table if you have occasion to do either. A sneeze is prevented by placing the finger firmly on the upper lip.

Never spit out bones, cherry pits, grape skins, etc. upon your plate. Quietly press them from your mouth upon the fork, and lay them upon the side of your plate.

Never allow the conversation at the table to drift into anything but chit-chat; the consideration of deep and abstruse principles will impair digestion.

Never permit yourself to engage in a heated argument at the table. Neither should you use gestures, nor illustrations made with a knife or fork upon the table-cloth.

True Ladies and Proper Gentlemen

Never pass forward to another the dish that has been handed to you, unless requested to do so; it may have been purposely designed for you, and passing it to another may give him or her what is not wanted.

Never put your feet so far under the table as to touch those of the person on the opposite side; neither should you curl them under nor at the side of your chair.

Never praise extravagantly every dish set before you; neither should you appear indifferent. Any article may have praise.

FIG. 12. GENTILITY IN THE DINING-ROOM.

The evidences of good breeding with a party of ladies and gentlemen seated about a table, who are accustomed to the usages of polite society, are many. Among these will be the fact that the table is very beautifully and artistically spread. This need not require much wealth, but good taste is necessary to set it handsomely.

Again, the company evince gentility by each assuming a genteel position while eating. It is not necessary that an elaborate toilet be worn at the table, but careful attention should always be given to neatness of personal appearance, however plain may be the dress which is worn.

Another evidence of good manners is the self-possession with which the company deport themselves throughout the meal.

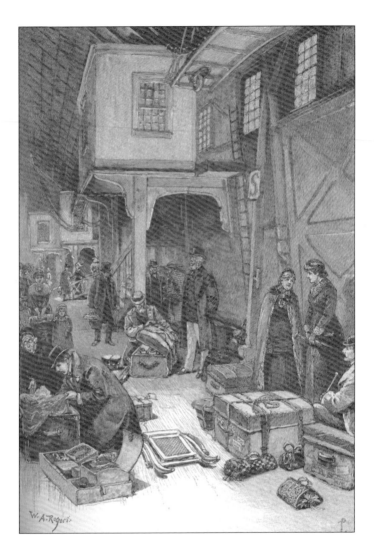

Bon Voyage!

The Art of Travel

By Elizabeth Bisland

There is a right way and a wrong way of doing everything, and the difference between the right way and the wrong way in travel is the whole space which lies between pleasure and disappointment. The proper method of travel is an art which may be learned perhaps only by personal experience, and some one else's personal experience is, on the whole, the cheaper sort. One personal experience can be summed up in a pair of phrases, which, rightly used, have the value of those magic amulets benignant witches present to young heroes when starting out to see the world, and which, applied to all difficulties, at once solved or removed them.

The first of these potential phrases is, "When in doubt use common-sense." The second grows naturally out of it: "Do in

Rome as do the Romans." In these two sayings lies the whole art of agreeable travelling . . .

So much of the pleasure of travel depends upon the physical condition of the traveller that such a paper as this had best begin with a few suggestions under the head of "Preparations." It is a difficult prescription to follow, but a good one, that one should begin a journey fresh and unfatigued. Packing should be well in hand twenty-four hours previous to setting out, and, under ordinary circumstances, a little forethought will obviate that furious hurry and scurry at the last moment which leaves the nerves tingling with excitement.

The question of luggage is to be governed, of course, by such considerations as length of absence, the season, and one's destination. My own opinion and experience is that a woman can travel comfortably to any distance, and to any climate, with one trunk, a dressing-bag, and a shawl-strap.

By natural sequence the next point to be considered is that of toilets. There is no need, in addressing American women, to inveigh against frowsy unkemptness in travelling—their tendency as a rule is toward "over-smartness;" but where a question of the quantity and weight of luggage is to be dealt with, it may be worth while to plan how an immaculate appearance and comfort are to be maintained out of trunks of small compass. . .

The many women who wear silk or wool tricot undergarments find them easily carried in small compass. Those who do not like this form of dress will discover that for long journeys there is nothing so satisfactory for underwear as silk. The original cost is rather large, but it proves an economy in the end, as clothes of the soft India (not China) silk are so easily laundered—requiring no starch—shed, instead of gathering, dust; do not conduct changes of temperature; and, keeping the body at an even temperature, are the greatest safeguards against colds. Nothing can be a greater luxury, in sea-sickness, or after a hot day in the cars, than to slip for the night into a silky garment which neither heats nor chills the skin, nor retains the dust and wrinkles of a previous wearing, as would cambric or linen.

The ideal travelling gown is undoubtedly a very plain tailor skirt and coat of some neutral-tinted serge or tweed, with a silk bodice, as it can stand the stress of weather, of sea-damps, and railway dust, is easy of fit, and can be adapted to the tropics by removing the coat, or adjusted to the arctic zone by the addition of furs. A simple and satisfactory adjunct is a black silk dress with two bodices—one adapted for evening. . .

It cannot be too much urged upon the traveller by land or by water, in temperate or tropic zone, that there should be no chance for exercise neglected. The change of air induces, as a rule, a more vigorous appetite, and the enforced sluggishness of long days on board vessel and car makes it difficult for the digestion to cope with its added task, the result being disorders which are apt to rob one of all pleasure and predispose one to colds and infection.

These suggestions apply to the case of the woman journeying under the escort of what is known as her natural protector, and treat principally of her physical comfort and well-being; but for the woman who sets forth into the world alone there are many matters still to be considered.

To the indolent, the timid, and the inexperienced among women there is something extremely terrifying in the thought of lonely wanderings, unaccompanied by some man to save trouble and bear the blame of mishaps; but there is, in reality, nothing to prevent a woman from seeing every civilized, and even semi-civilized, country in the world without other protection than her own modesty and good sense. There is a vast amount of chivalry and tenderness distributed in the hearts of men, and while the woman who goes guarded may be quite unaware of it, because nothing in her case calls it forth, the chivalry is there, and ready for almost unlimited draughts upon its patience, devotion, and sympathy. In all accidents by land or water the first thought of those in authority is the safety of the women, and while all yet goes smoothly the very defencelessness of a lonely woman appears to put every man upon his honor, and make him feel, in a certain sense, responsible for her comfort and enjoyment. That women travelling alone have at times painful experiences cannot be denied, but I boldly assert that in nine cases out of ten it is due wholly and solely to their own fault. A few have been so warned against the wiles of a wicked world that they are unable to discriminate between an honest desire to be of use and mere vulgar effrontery, and reward courteous attentions with suspicious rudeness. Still another cause of difficulty is an embarassed timidity in cases where instant repression is needed; and a lack of courageous dignity in the face of insolence.

The woman who is cool-headed, courteous, and self-reliant, can travel around the world in every direction and find no word or look to daunt or distress her. Indeed if her manners be sweetly gracious and dignified she will find all lands full of brave cavaliers who will spring to gratify her smallest request, who will see and meet her needs before they are put into words, and who cheerfully will imperil and even yield up their lives in her defense and to insure her safety . . .

Impertinence is not the only matter with which the solitary woman must deal; she must be alert, accurate, and quick-witted, and while she is sure to find assistance she must act as if she did not count upon it, and take all possible precautions for herself . . .

It is the gentleman who sits at the receipt of custom who fills with vague alarm many a gentle female soul, but experience usually robs him of all terrors. Strangely enough, England, which is supposed to be entirely free from any protective measures, is a most troublesome port to enter. Brandy, cologne, silver plate, tobacco and the Tauchnitz novels are not permitted to enter the tight little island, and it is generally some well-behaved, eminently conventional matron who is most sharply questioned as to the presence of tobacco and brandy in her trunks, and has her stockings, under-linen, and bonnets tossed madly about in the search for contraband means of distribution. On the Continent more discrimination is shown, and for the most part the officers of the *douane* discern at a glance whether one is likely to have diamonds concealed in one's boot-heels, or owes the rich contours of one's figure to tightly rolled consignments of lace.[16] The slightest reluctance to have one's belongings searched, however, at once arouses suspicion, and only the cheerful and prompt handing over of keys achieves the much-to-be-desired mere lifting and closing of the lid. My own experience leads me to believe that the most courteous and kindly of customs officials are those in the Port of New York—and that even under the McKinley tariff regulations; but memory preserves in the amber of gratitude one gentle-hearted Gaul, who, looking into the weary eyes of a lonely woman newly arrived in Paris at eight o'clock in the evening, was moved to real compassion and chalked with his mystic sign four large boxes without word or question . . .

All directions and suggestions to travellers must of necessity be vague and general; each voyage, like each life, is individual and unique; but common sense and good temper alike each are the two safest guides and most agreeable traveling companions.

---

[16] Imported lace was taxed highly in the late nineteenth-century, and therefore a popular item for smuggling. One popular method among women smugglers was to wrap many yards of lace around their legs underneath their skirts. Some of the earliest women customs officials in New York were matrons employed to take suspected woman smugglers aside and check under their skirts for contraband.

SEARCHING A FEMALE SMUGGLER.

Etiquette of Traveling

The reader will call to mind people who always appear at ease when they are traveling. Investigation will prove that those individuals have usually had a wide experience in journeying, and an extensive acquaintance with the world. The experienced traveler has learned the necessity of always being on time, of having baggage checked early, of purchasing a ticket before entering the cars, and of procuring a seat in a good location before the car is full.

The inexperienced traveler is readily known by his flurry and mistakes. He is likely to be behind time, and he is likely to be an hour too early. For want of explicit direction, his baggage often fails to reach the train in time, or does not come at all. His trunks, from lack of strength, are liable to be easily broken. In his general confusion, when he buys a ticket he neglects to place it where it will be secure, and consequently loses it. He forgets a portion of his baggage, and thus in a dozen ways he is likely to be in trouble. If the person be a lady who is unacquainted with travel, she reveals the fact by a general impatience, restlessness, and absent-mindedness. In her want of self-possession she forgets several things she had intended to bring, and her continual fault-finding at flies, dust, heat, delay and other trials, all betray the fact that she has not heretofore been accustomed to these difficulties.

The following suggestions relating to railway traveling may be of service:

Whenever you contemplate a journey, consider carefully what route you want to take, and decide it definitely. Learn accurately what time the train leaves, and provide yourself with a table giving the running time of the road, stations on the way, etc., which will save you the trouble of asking many questions.

If you desire to ride in a sleeping-car, secure your berth a day or two previous to the time of going, in order that you may be in time to take your choice. The most desirable sections are in the center of the car, away from the annoyance of dust, drafts of air and sudden noises resulting from opening and closing doors.

At least a day before you go, consider carefully what baggage you need to take, and have it packed. Take just as little as possible. Have your trunks very secure, and pack all articles of baggage in such a manner that they cannot shake and thus be broken.

Provide among your baggage necessary toilet articles—a linen wrap to exclude the dust from your finer clothing, and a small amount of reading-matter with very coarse type. See that your baggage is perfectly in order, and an hour before you start engage an authorized expressman to take your baggage to the depot. State very distinctly where you want the baggage taken, and for what train. It is also a wise provision to have your trunk labeled with a card bearing your name and destination.

Take the number of the expressman, ascertain his charge, and withhold payment until he has assisted in finding baggage, and has aided in getting it checked at the depot. Be very sure that your watch or clock is perfectly correct with railroad time, and that you, half an hour before the starting time of the train, arrive at the depot, buy a ticket, and take your seat in the car. You are probably early enough to take your choice of location in the seats.

Having selected a seat, it is customary to deposit the satchel, umbrella or some article of wearing-apparel in the same, should you not be ready to occupy it; and it is etiquette for anyone finding a seat so occupied to look further.

You should carry just as little baggage into the car as possible, and all separate pieces should have your name plainly written or printed upon them, which will secure their being forwarded to you in case they are left upon the seat.

Having paid for one ticket, you are entitled to only one seat. It shows selfishness, therefore, when the coach is quite full to deposit a large amount of baggage in the surrounding seats and occupy three or four, and engage in reading, while others look in vain for a place to sit down.

It is courtesy for a gentleman when sitting alone to offer the vacant seat beside himself to a lady who may be unattended. He will also give his seat to two ladies, or a lady and gentleman who desire to sit together, and take a seat elsewhere. Such attention will often be a great kindness, while the individual bestowing it may suffer but little inconvenience.

What to Avoid When Traveling

A lady and gentleman should avoid evidences of undue familiarity in the presence of strangers. Couples who may evince a silly affection by overfondling of each other in public make themselves appear ridiculous to all who may see them.

People with weak eyes should avoid reading on the train, and those having weak lungs should avoid much talking, as an undue effort will be required to talk above the noise of the train.

Passengers should avoid eating at irregular times on the journey, and gentlemen should avoid smoking in the presence of those to whom it may be offensive.

Avoid undue haste and excitement when traveling, by forethought. Have a plan matured, and when the time comes to act you will know what to do, and with self-possession you accomplish your work very much better.

Avoid wearing laces, velvets, or any articles that naturally accumulate and hold dust. Excessive finery or a lavish display of jewelry are in bad taste on extended journeys. Before commencing a journey, consider carefully what will be most suitable to wear, and study how little baggage may be taken.

Conduct for Gentlemen When Traveling With Ladies

If the gentleman is an authorized escort he will, if an old acquaintance, accompany the lady in his charge from her residence to the depot. If the acquaintance is of short duration, it will be sufficient to meet her at the depot in ample time to

purchase tickets and see that her baggage is checked, while she remains in the sitting-room at the station.

Arrangements being made, he will secure her a seat upon the train, will find a place for packages, will attend to her wants in adjusting the window, and will aim to put her entirely at ease.

In getting on and off the train, the gentleman will care for all parcels and see that nothing is left. He will assist the lady into the coach or omnibus before getting in himself, and in getting out he will precede her, and afterwards turn and help her carefully down.

He should purchase the needed confections or literature on the train. He should be fruitful in the introduction of topics that will enliven, amuse and instruct the lady, if she is inclined to be reticent; and at her journey's end he should go with her to her home, or the place where she is to stop. He may call next day, and if the acquaintance seems desirable it may be continued. The gentleman should be very careful not to continue his visits unless certain that they are acceptable.

If a hotel be the point of destination, the gentleman will accompany the lady to the parlor. He will then secure for her a room, and leave her in care of a waiter; her desire being probably to proceed to her apartments at once, where she will remove the dust and travel stains of the journey, and meet him again at a concerted hour in the parlor.

Ladies and gentlemen who are strangers, being thrown into the company of each other for a long journey, need not necessarily refuse to speak to each other. While the lady should be guarded, acquaintance may be made with certain reserve.

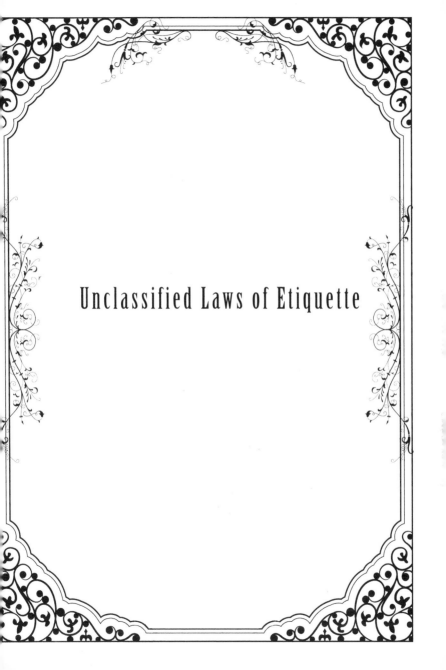

Unclassified Laws of Etiquette

Unclassified Laws of Etiquette

Never exaggerate.

Never point at another.

Never betray a confidence.

Never wantonly frighten others.

Never leave home with unkind words.

Never neglect to call upon your friends.

Never laugh at the misfortunes of others.

Never give a promise that you do not fulfill.

True Ladies and Proper Gentlemen

Never speak much of your own performances.

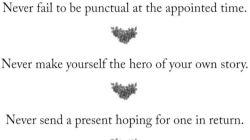

Never fail to be punctual at the appointed time.

Never make yourself the hero of your own story.

Never send a present hoping for one in return.

Never pick the teeth or clean the nails in company.

Never fail to give a polite answer to a civil question.

Never question a servant or a child about family matters.

Never read letters which you may find addressed to others.

Never fail, if a gentleman, of being civil, and polite to ladies.

Never call attention to the features or form of any one present.

Never refer to a gift you have made or favor you have rendered.

Never associate with bad company. Have good company or none.

Never look over the shoulder of another who is reading or writing.

Never seem to notice a scar, deformity, or defect of any one present.

Never arrest the attention of an acquaintance by a touch. Speak to him.

Never punish your child for a fault to which you are addicted yourself.

Never answer questions in general company that have been put to others.

True Ladies and Proper Gentlemen

Never, when traveling abroad, be over-boastful in praise of your own country.

Never call a new acquaintance by the Christian name unless requested to do so.

Never lend an article you have borrowed unless you have permission to do so.

Never attempt to draw the attention of the company constantly upon yourself.

Never exhibit anger, impatience or excitement when an accident happens.

Never pass between two persons who are talking together, without an apology.

Never enter a room noisily; never fail to close the door after you, and never slam it.

Never forget that if you are faithful in a few things, you may be ruler over many.

Never exhibit too great familiarity with the new acquaintance; you may give offense.

Never will a gentleman allude to conquests which he may have made with ladies.

Never fail to offer the easiest and best seat in the room to an invalid, an elderly person, or a lady.

Never neglect to perform the commission which the friend entrusted to you. You must not forget.

Never send your guest, who is accustomed to a warm room, off into a cold, damp, spare bed to sleep.

Never enter a room filled with people without a slight bow to the general company when first entering.

True Ladies and Proper Gentlemen

Never fail to answer an invitation, either personally or by letter, within a week after the invitation is received.

Never accept of favors and hospitalities without rendering an exchange of civilities when opportunity offers.

Never cross the legs and put out one foot in the street-car or places where it will trouble others when passing by.

Never fail to tell the truth. If truthful you get your reward. You will get your punishment if you deceive.

Never borrow money and neglect to pay. If you do you will soon be known as a person of no business integrity.

Never write to another asking for information, or a favor of any kind, without enclosing a postage stamp for the reply.

Never compel a woman with an infant in arms to stand while you retain your seat.

Never fail to say kind and encouraging words to those whom you meet in distress. Your kindness may lift them out of their despair.

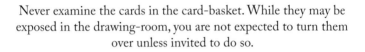

Never refuse to receive an apology. You may not revive friendship, but courtesy will require, when an apology is offered, that you accept it.

Never examine the cards in the card-basket. While they may be exposed in the drawing-room, you are not expected to turn them over unless invited to do so.

Never, when walking arm in arm with a lady, be continually changing and going to the other side, because of the change of corners. It shows too much attention to form.

Never should the lady accept of expensive gifts at the hands of a gentleman not related or engaged to her. Gifts of flowers, books, music or confectionary may be accepted.

Never insult another by harsh words when applied to for a favor. Kind words do not cost much, and yet they may carry untold happiness to the one to whom they are spoken.

Never fail to speak kindly. If a merchant, and you address your clerk; if an overseer, and you address your workmen; if in any position where you exercise authority, you show yourself to be a gentleman by your pleasant mode of address.

Never attempt to convey the impression that you are a genius by imitating the faults of distinguished men. Because certain great men were poor penmen, wore long hair, or had other peculiarities, it does not follow that you will be great by imitating their eccentricities.

Never give all your pleasant words and smiles to strangers. The kindest words and the sweetest smiles should be reserved for home. Home should be our heaven.

Bibliography by Piece

The Story of an Old Letter
Peterson's Magazine. Philadelphia: August 1890, pages 158–161.

Advice on Writing Love Letters, Answering Personal Ads, Courtship,
and Marriage
Hill, Thomas E. *Hill's Manual of Social and Business Forms . . .* Chicago:
Hill Standard Book Co., 1891, pages 110–116.

Etiquette of Courtship
Hill, Thomas E. *Hill's Manual of Social and Business Forms . . .* Chicago:
Hill Standard Book Co., 1891, pages 110–116, 164–168.

Etiquette between Husbands and Wives
Hill, Thomas E. *Hill's Manual of Social and Business Forms . . .* Chicago:
Hill Standard Book Co., 1891, page 167.

The Wife's Duty
Hill, Thomas E. *Hill's Manual of Social and Business Forms . . .* Chicago:
Hill Standard Book Co., 1891, page 167.

The Husband's Duty
Hill, Thomas E. *Hill's Manual of Social and Business Forms . . .* Chicago:
Hill Standard Book Co., 1891, page 167.

Betsey and I Are Out
Hill, Thomas E. *Hill's Manual of Social and Business Forms . . .* Chicago:
Hill Standard Book Co., 1891, page 542.

How Betsey and I Made Up
Hill, Thomas E. *Hill's Manual of Social and Business Forms . . .*
    Chicago: Hill Standard Book Co., 1891, page 542.

Attractive Physical Appearance
Hill, Thomas E. *Hill's Manual of Social and Business Forms . . .* Chicago:
    Hill Standard Book Co., 1891, pages 176–181.

Etiquette in the Home: Parents and Children
Hill, Thomas E. *Hill's Manual of Social and Business Forms . . .* Chicago:
    Hill Standard Book Co., 1891, pages 174–175.

My Step-Children: An Echo from the Halls of Vassar College
Good Housekeeping, June 23, 1888, Springfield, Massachusetts, pages
    77–78.

Classroom Etiquette
Hill, Thomas E. *Hill's Manual of Social and Business Forms . . .* Chicago:
    Hill Standard Book Co., 1891, pages 173–174.

Etiquette of Shopping
Hill, Thomas E. *Hill's Manual of Social and Business Forms . . .* Chicago:
    Hill Standard Book Co., 1891, page 151.

Etiquette of the Street: Rules of Conduct to be Observed
Hill, Thomas E. *Hill's Manual of Social and Business Forms . . .* Chicago:
    Hill Standard Book Co., 1891, page 182.

Modern Improvements
Greene, Belle C. *Adventures of an Old* Maid. J.S. Ogilvie Publishing
    Company: New York, 1881, pages 127–129.

Etiquette of Conversation
Hill, Thomas E. *Hill's Manual of Social and Business Forms* . . . Chicago: Hill Standard Book Co., 1891, pages 152–153.

At Other People's Convenience: "A Whole Week Put Out of Join for a Twenty Minutes' Call."
Good Housekeeping No. 131, May 10, 1890: Springfield, Massachusetts, page 14.

Etiquette of Calling
Hill, Thomas E. *Hill's Manual of Social and Business Forms* . . . Chicago: Hill Standard Book Co., 1891, pages 148–149.

The Art of Travel
Bisland, Elizabeth. *The Woman's Book Volume 1*. Charles Scribner's Sons: New York, 1894, pages 371–400.

Etiquette of Traveling
Hill, Thomas E. *Hill's Manual of Social and Business Forms* . . . Chicago: Hill Standard Book Co., 1891, pages 168–169.

Unclassified Laws of Etiquette
Hill, Thomas E. *Hill's Manual of Social and Business Forms* . . . Chicago: Hill Standard Book Co., 1891, page 183.

Illustration Credits

The illustrations in this book originally appeared in the following publications:

Illustration on page xii, Masson, Tom. *A Corner in Women.* New York: Moffat, Yard & Co., page 61 (Illustration by R.M. Crosby. Original title, "When You Are Married.")

Illustration on page 2, *Peterson's Magazine*, February 1890. Philadelphia Vol. XCVII No. 2, Supplement. (Original title, "A Troubled Hour.")

Illustration on page 11, Masson, Tom. *A Corner in Women.* New York: Moffat, Yard & Co., p. 55 (Illustration by R.M. Crosby. Original title, "When You Are Engaged.")

Illustration on page 12, Hill, Thomas E. *Hill's Manual of Social and Business Forms . . .* Chicago: Hill Standard Book Co., 1891. p. 21

Illustration on page 17, Talmage, T. DeWeitt. *Social Dynamite: Or, the Wickedness of Modern Society.* Chicago: Standard Publishing Company, p. 156

Illustration on page 21, *Harper's New Monthly Magazine*, September 1870. Vol. XLI, No. CCXLIV. page 555 (Original title of illustration: "The Meeting")

Illustration on page 26, Masson, Tom. *A Corner in Women.* New York: Moffat, Yard & Co., p. 49 (Illustration by T.K. Hannah Jr. Original title, "You Didn't Wait.")

Illustration on page 32, *The Argosy*, December 1889. (Frontispiece. Illustration by W. Small. Original title, "It is my brother - it is Rex.")

Illustration on page 33, Talmage, T. DeWeitt. *Social Dynamite: Or, the Wickedness of Modern Society.* Chicago: Standard Publishing Company, p. 76

Illustration on page 37, Masson, Tom. *A Corner in Women.* New York: Moffat, Yard & Co., p. 58 (Illustration by John Cecil Clay. Original title, "The First Kiss.")

Illustration on page 40, *Petersons Magazine,* Philadelphia: May 1890, Vol XCVII No. 5, insert. (Original title, "'I will not help you,' she said.")

Illustration on page 43, *Petersons Magazine,* Philadelphia: October 1890, Vol. XCVIII, No 4, page 320

Illustration on page 47, Green, Belle C. *Adventures of An Old Maid.* New York: J.S. Ogilvie Publishing Company, 1886, page 131

Illustration on page 52, *The Blunders of A Bashful Man.* New York: J.S. Ogilvie Publishing Company, 1886, Cover

Illustration on page 56, *Godey's Lady's Book.* December 1890. Philadelphia: Vol CXIX, No714. page 449

Illustration on page 62, Wiggin, Kate Douglas. *The Birds' Christmas Carol.* Boston and New York: Houghton Mifflin Company, 1888, frontispiece.

Illustration on page 82, *The Cottage Hearth.* Boston: February 1888, Vol XIV, page 56.

Illustration on page 86, Wiggin, Kate Douglas. *The Birds' Christmas Carol.* Boston and New York: Houghton Mifflin Company, 1888, page 39. (Original title, "I want ter see how yer goin' to behave.")

Illustration on page 89, Wiggin, Kate Douglas. *The Birds' Christmas Carol.* Boston and New York: Houghton Mifflin Company, 1888, page 7. (Original title, "She is a little Christmas child.")

Illustration on page 92, Hill, Thomas E. *Hill's Manual of Social and Business Forms...* Chicago: Hill Standard Book Co., 1891. p. 173.

Illustration on page 94, *Petersons Magazine.* Philadelphia: January, 1890. Vol XCVII. No 1. Fashion insert.

Illustration on page 106, *Petersons Magazine.* Philadelphia: December, 1890. Vol XCVIII, No. 6, fashion insert.

Illustration on page 108, Hill, Thomas E. *Hill's Manual of Social and Business Forms...* Chicago: Hill Standard Book Co., 1891. p. 145.

Illustration on page 110, Hill, Thomas E. *Hill's Manual of Social and Business Forms . . .* Chicago: Hill Standard Book Co., 1891. p. 151.

Illustration on page 113, *The Wheelman.* June, 1883, p. 164.

Illustration on page 118, *Godey's Lady's Book.* Philadelphia: October 1889, Vol. CXIX No. 712, fashion insert.

Illustration on page 120, *Life.* April 27, 1916 Vol. 67, No. 1748, page 790. (Original title, "Dinner in the Suburbs.")

Illustration on page 134, *Harper's New Monthly Magazine*, July 1870. Vol. XLI, No. CCXLII. page 236 (Original title of illustration: "The Arrival")

Illustration on page 136, *Godey's Lady's Book,* Philadelphia: January, 1890, Vol CXX, No. 715, p.10

Illustrations on p. 141, 142, Hill, Thomas E. *Hill's Manual of Social and Business Forms…* Chicago: Hill Standard Book Co., p. 150

Illustration on p. 150, Hill, Thomas E. *Hill's Manual of Social and Business Forms…* Chicago: Hill Standard Book Co., p. 148

Illustration on p. 151, Hill, Thomas E. *Hill's Manual of Social and Business Forms…* Chicago: Hill Standard Book Co., p. 149.

Illustration on p. 153, Hill, Thomas E. *Hill's Manual of Social and Business Forms…* Chicago: Hill Standard Book Co., p. 158.

Illustration on page 162, *Harper's New Monthly Magazine,* New York: Harper & Brothers. June 1884, No. 409, page 43. (Original title, "Inspection of Cabin Passengers' Baggage on the Dock.")

Illustration on page 164, *The Woman's Book Volume I.* New York: Charles Scribner's Sons. 1894, page 387. (Original title, "The End of the Voyage.")

Illustration on page 169, *Harper's New Monthly Magazine,* New York: Harper & Brothers. June 1884, No. 409, page 45. (Original title, "Searching a Female Smuggler.")

Illustration on page 170, *Godey's Lady's Book*. Philadelphia: October 1889, Vol. CXIX No. 712. page 274.

Illustration on p. 173, Hill, Thomas E. *Hill's Manual of Social and Business Forms...* Chicago: Hill Standard Book Co., p. 159

Illustration on page 176, *The Argosy*. November 1889, page 401. (Original title, "Going up the Eiffel Tower.")

Illustration on page 179, *Godey's Magazine*. Philadelphia: September, 1889. Vol. CXIX, No. 711 p.183

Illustration on page 187, *Godey's Lady's Book*. Philadelphia: December 1889, Vol. CXIX, No. 714, Fashion insert.

Index

Godey's Fashion Plates

GODEY'S FASHIONS.

FOR DESCRIPTION SEE FASHION DEPARTMENT.

September 1889

GODEY'S FASHIONS.
FOR DESCRIPTION SEE FASHION DEPARTMENT.

October 1889

GODEY'S FASHIONS.

FOR DESCRIPTION SEE FASHION DEPARTMENT.

November 1889

GODEY'S FASHIONS.

FOR DESCRIPTION SEE FASHION DEPARTMENT.

January 1890

GODEY'S FASHIONS.

FOR DESCRIPTION SEE FASHION DEPARTMENT.

February 1890

GODEYS FASHIONS.

FOR DESCRIPTION SEE FASHION DEPARTMENT.

March 1890

GODEY'S FASHIONS.

FOR DESCRIPTION SEE FASHION DEPARTMENT.

April 1890